CRACK IN THE DOOR
A Memoir

Roberta Swann

MadHat Press
Asheville, North Carolina

MadHat Press
MadHat Incorporated
PO Box 8364, Asheville, NC 28814

Copyright © 2017 Roberta Swann
All rights reserved

The Library of Congress has assigned
this edition a Control Number of
2017951749

ISBN 978-1-941196-54-0 (paperback)

Text by Roberta Swann
Cover design by Marc Vincenz

www.madhat-press.com

First Printing

CRACK IN THE DOOR
A Memoir

For Brian

Table of Contents

One

Here and Elsewhere	3
Losing Streak (1)	17
Losing Streak (2)	19
Pain	38
Chronic Fatigue Syndrome	40
Rita	43
December 21, 2011	49
Window	50
More	52
Superstitions	54
Beckett	55
Jump Rope	56
David Blaine	57
A Crack in the Door	60
No More Sorrows	61

Two

About Time	67
Goodland	75
The Day the Yoga Died	81
Discounted	87
Community Service	92

Three

A Little Bit about the American Jazz Orchestra	99
John Lewis	101
Max Roach	104

Playing It by Ear	107
Recycling	110
Bartleby Redux	112
Bartleby, Again	114
Holidays	115
House	125
A Seat on the Bus	134
Miss Brooklyn	136
She Has Some Nerve	138
There's Always Free Cheese in a Mousetrap	139
Red and Blue	140
Birthday	141
Thrushes	143
Happy Days	144
Pooh	146
Owl	148
An American Classic	149
Trash Talk	151
Staying Alive	152
Windfall	153
About the Author	155

One

Here and Elsewhere

She raged over the phone, calling me an idiot and bastard. Her son-in-law was worse, a moron who did my dirty work, in this case calling the assisted living facility where my 92-year-old mother now resides to find out what's what. "I need more money for tips. I'm not getting any service." Tipping is prohibited. A small sign in the lobby says so. We indulged her. Why not, if this made her happy? But I'd just filled her wallet. Was she being extorted? The authorities got right on it. The staff denied accepting gratuities. There was no one to chew out. Had my mother deceived us?

She's not an easy mother, not one for kissing and moves away if you touch her. Affection spreads germs. I've rationalized she's colorful, not cold, that her undemonstrative ways have spared me *kenahoras* and the evil eye. Even now, I'm not certain what makes her tick. When I was ten, I found a clock in the refrigerator she put there by mistake. Whenever I lost a sock or my homework I'd look there first. During her older years she kept a glass jar filled with silverware in the fridge. Even she didn't know why.

I plead for reason over the phone. I haven't a knack for saying no. On my knee I'm nervously ironing a $20 bill I used as a bookmark. She spews insult after boiling insult. The violent silences are worse. I don't want her to hang up on me again, and check my impulse to retaliate. She sounds like my mother, but worse. Mood swings like this have happened before. I have to wait for the light to change, and brace myself.

"What have you ever done for me?" she asks.

Does she want a stenographic record? All the gifts I give her get a "put it over there." Alone, she'll scrutinize each and say I spent too much.

"Too much, I've lived too much."

"Maybe you should stop all the vitamins you make me buy."

I lighten up on her account, for the sake of the wide Russian aide filling the door, who gives me a look I don't care for. The place is overrun by Soviet specialists who, in addition to monthly rent that would cover the cost of any Hilton, charge by the hour for assisting the elderly who need even more assistance than assisted living affords. In a moment of weakness we once asked my mother if she'd like to come and live with us. "I'd rather be dead," she said.

*

My mother was homebound for ten years. I hadn't realized I was a "caretaker" until she called me one. I became a connoisseur of medical centers and pain clinics. It was my moral obligation to look after her. I rearranged my schedule to fit her needs. Illness was a foreign country I navigated as I went along. There was satisfaction gaining practical skills to manage one crisis after another. Much to my surprise, I had it in me.

One morning I called and could barely hear her. *Come*, she said, and I did. My husband left the class he was teaching at Cooper Union and we met at the garage. Crossing the Brooklyn Bridge, I thought this was it. She was collapsed in bed, barely breathing, when I let myself in. I pulled out a card of emergency numbers that was embedded in my wallet and dialed Hatzolah. The next number down was Adath Israel Burial Society, which my mother had paid dues to for the past forty years so she could rest beside my father at Beth David Cemetery. The intercom sounded five minutes later.

Three men came in with a stretcher. One took vital signs and asked questions. The other two were on phones, making arrangements in Hebrew. I was calmed by their expertise and ancient Hasidic looks. I rode shotgun with my mother and one medic to Maimonides Hospital. When we reached the ER, the other familiar face met us, conveying my mother through crowds and staying with her until we were served and put in the system. Doctors in green scrubs ran relays. I did not fall apart. I told my mother she was in good hands. She neither shed a tear nor showed fear. The Hatzolah men refused the money I offered and left. Our one distraction was six policemen guarding a raving, drug-addled gunshot victim who'd just held up a bodega. Every gain was hard-won: a blanket, a bedpan, an aide and finally a doctor who quickly administered blood. Twenty-seven pints brought her back. Twelve hours later she was moved to a bed on the sixth floor. She stayed for a month and transferred to The Jewish Home and Hospital to rehabilitate for another month. Everything was wrong. The infections that almost killed her subsided. The pancreatic tumor stayed. She was too frail for surgery.

*

"I'm alive," she responds when I ask her how she feels. We're sitting on the terrace and she asks the names of trees. I'm encouraged, and encouraging her to mingle, to strike up some friendships.

"What for? Everyone is dying. Three last week." She holds up fingers to confirm the latest tally. "I rode the elevator with a woman every day. So I asked her name. She said it was pointless, I'd forget. The next time we met she told me."

"So what's her name?" I asked.

"I forgot," she laughed. I laughed too, holding on to the happy day. "We had a nice visit," she said.

*

My mother has never told me: I love you. She says talk is cheap, a cliché you can't counter. I grew up with her notion that only she would tell me the truth, that friends aren't family and people are jealous. "Blood is thicker than water," she'd often say. If you wanted to know how you looked in a marked-down dress, she was your man. She never pulled punches.

*

She's had a hard life. My father died at thirty-eight. My sister is retarded. My mother worked for forty years. She called me a little *mamzer* (devil). I mistakenly heard "mambo star" and danced crazy cha-cha steps around the table, breaking the china centerpiece. I saved my allowance to make amends, and replaced it with a wooden wheelbarrow full of plastic fruit, hoping that our kitchen would now look like everyone else's.

*

My father was handsome. Everyone said so. He was a gambler and pool-shark who took me to the track and let me bet on horses, where I discovered I had a lucky number: 3. When he walked down the street his shoes made noise. I'd leave my friends and jump rope for his hand. Who needs to be called in one, two, three, when you had a father who entered you into a beauty contest? I wore a two-piece swimsuit patterned with one sailboat every two fishes. I sang "Que sera sera" just like Doris Day. The winners were selected by applause. My father jumped from his seat that slapped like thunder and ran down the center aisle of the auditorium encouraging, "Clap! Clap!" They did, but not enough, because I lost. Later, driving home, he kept taking his eyes off the road to look at me.

"You're beautiful," he pronounced. "They're crazy."
I was also a little chubby.

*

My mother's suite at Harbor View has a view of Sheepshead Bay she's too short to see. The windows are too high. Sitting on her bed, sun whitens her hair even more. She likes her room. "It's very light." The best they have. But the chocolates I bought are lousy. O'Henrys are good enough.

"Who needs Lady Godiva? You're too old to wear your hair in a ponytail."

"You're only old once," I joke.

But she's serious. She doesn't like my skinny jeans: "Who wears boots in the summer?"

My perfume makes her sneeze. I defend each designer, but my mother takes exception. She gets on her walker, opens the armoire and starts tossing grapefruits, big as cannonballs, into my "stupid Prada bag."

"What you need to eat is more fruit."

She selects a champagne truffle from the box. "Peanut M & Ms are good too."

*

To have a father who thinks you're more and a mother who thinks you're less leaves you unbalanced. So I hang onto my father. Every lucky penny I stoop for brings me protection. My mother was left penniless after he died. When she went to the United Jewish Appeal for financial aid, the man in charge told her money wasn't everything, and turned her down. She never cried in front of me, but I could hear her weeping all night long. She took a civil-service exam and started working for the Board of Ed, climbing to administrator in charge of payroll. I met a teacher at a party once who told me my mother cleared an advance on his salary. "Nobody ever gave *me* a dime," my mother recounted when I told her.

*

The TV stays tuned to Channel 13 because she can't activate the remote, aiming it at walls and ceiling. When she lived in her apartment, my husband changed light bulbs every time we visited because she was afraid of suddenly being left in the dark. She's unmechanical, but won't acknowledge it. Brian was good for pushing the mattress back into place, hanging frames, fixing her tape deck. I was good for shopping. She wouldn't trust him to get the right flavor of oatmeal. She hardly trusted me. We're sitting in her room now at Harbor View, and she is again resurrecting my bad behavior for my husband, who over the years she's grown to like, as much as she likes anyone. He feels for me and asks her if she can remember any good things. "No," she answers flatly. Nothing impresses her. I worked briefly as a fashion model. She came to a show. The designer said I was just the right fit for his clothes. She said I looked better in photos. And stood in a corner backstage, inspecting seams. We go over bank statements. She spots a check I haven't recorded and calls me stupid. "You're not a business person." She eyes my husband, hoping he'll join in. But he's staring at seagulls. She accuses him of being bored. "Tell me, how can students respect a professor who dresses in jeans?" He shrugs. He's used to this. She likes men who dress like the captains of cruise ships she used to go on. "You're hopeless," she smiles, and for a moment we enjoy her better nature.

*

I phone so she can wish me Happy Birthday. She's glad I got her early so she can forget about it. But she's in good spirits and reminds me of the treasures she made of my ankle chains and charm bracelets I wanted to return to finished boyfriends. "Why should you?" She used to wear a necklace with my nickname, "Fanny," in gold cursive letters, from a lifeguard who thought I had a nice one.

*

My aunt Jeanette, her baby sister, was another oddball, who called the cops to report a bear in her Brooklyn bathroom. They came with firemen and nets and caught a rat she insisted was a bear until the day she died of breast cancer. When I was diagnosed with breast cancer, the doctor took a family history. "Only an aunt," I said. "But we weren't close." "You should have told me sooner," he said.

*

I was in Rome, abroad and in love for the first time, with my not-then husband. He had a lot of Italian friends and we went everywhere. My observations were not in the guide books. Moses didn't look Jewish. Money seemed beside the point. I'd buy bread, hand over a bill, and get a banana for change because there was no coin to cover the difference. I phoned my mother. I told her I'd just spent Sunday with Roberto Rossellini. "Big deal," she said. I hung up and left a stack of *gettoni* I never used in the booth.

*

But now she is really confused. She's forgetting her past. "Don't get upset," she begins in a low voice. "Tell me, what happened to my sister?" I tell her Jeanette is long dead and supply details she doesn't remember. She cared for her sister all through her illness. After the funeral, she sold her house and put her affairs in order. She never complained. She always did the work. She left each morning, took a two-hour bus trip and got the hard stuff done. She's forgotten which vitamins to take when, and that Brian and I used to have a house in the country where she picked blueberries and where she broke her wrist. "Remember, Mom, when we went hiking and you fell into a ditch taking a pee?"

*

My mother lived in a one-bedroom apartment in Trump Village, the first family dwelling the Trump family built. She liked to say how big her apartment was, how her livingroom was nicer and bigger than ours. When it came time to dismantle, it took many painful months. There was no easy way out. My husband and I just did it. At first, I let sadness creep in. I cradled every object. Took time-outs for tears. It was the stockpiles of canned salmon that sobered me, so much the closet smelled like low tide. Some of the sardines could be carbon-dated. There were fifty rolls of toilet paper she said she was always out of that fell in an avalanche on my head. There were drawers of new leather gloves she kept for best and never wore. Bags and bags of wool her hands grew too arthritic to knit with. Empty jam jars and plastic bags spread like kudzu. The only thing we took was the large leather sofa I had bought her. It turned out to be too big to fit into her elevator going down, though it had fitted in on the way up. We tipped the two moving men well to carry it down the 13 floors. In the end I threw most of her things away. All that's gone stays in my mind, as vivid as the boxes of photographs I saved.

*

My sister Rita and I shared a room as children. I hardly remember her. I was always looking in the mirror. Even my father couldn't stand that. She was borderline retarded, special-needs, "slow" according to who was making the assessment. But she was fast enough to run away from home at 16. My mother hired a detective who found her living in a black ghetto with an old man named Kelly whose kindness included cooking and caring for her. When Kelly died, she went to a group home where she met Ray. With the help of social workers, they set up house. They've been together in this common-law way for thirty years, managing life in slow motion. Except when my sister went on a gambling spree, forgot to pay the rent, cashed savings bonds lawlessly and wound up living on the streets, before my mother found her and took her in. For years, every time my mom and I called her, we assumed it was Surf Manor where she went to live under the protection of state supervision. My mother had peace of mind. Rita was safe and settled in. We accepted her explanation that she was there under the provision that she had no family. So we never visited and always met at my mother's apartment. A month after I moved my mother into Harbor View my sister called. She was crying. "I live with Ray," she finally admitted. I was shocked. She told me how good he was to her, how well he cooks rice and beans and now she's had a husband like everyone else. Still, they are an unlikely pair. My sister is a heavy, Jewish, childlike woman with a large head and missing front teeth who shuffles only short distances with a cane. Ray is a small, slender, nice-looking Puerto Rican who wears powder-blue three-piece polyester suits, who with proper medication hides his schizophrenia. Every time I phone he says the same thing:

"Hello, hello. Rita, it's your sister. God bless you. God bless Brian. If you're OK I'm OK. Here's Rita."

Medication can only do so much.

*

The deception was so clever, so elaborate and I so stupid, my head reels, even now. She stayed at Surf Manor only for a few months and got back together with Ray. All along, when Ray answered the phone, I thought it was "Carol," her black roommate she got along so well with, who had a deep voice and sounded like a man. When I asked her to do this or that, her supervisor "Marie" would not permit it. For years, my preoccupation was with her trips to the dentist to get her teeth reinstated. The progress report was slow. The bus broke down, Marie was visiting her sister in PR, the dentist died. She had another in Staten Island, but he was only there once a month. If she didn't care about her teeth, why was I driving myself nuts? All her excuses were irritating but believable. It never occurred to me she was cagey. When bearer bonds disappeared, I'd discovered she'd cashed them.

"Mom gave them to me," she swore, crying over the phone. "I'm a liar, but I'm not a thief."

As it turned out, she was both.

*

My father's family all live in Montreal. They took to calling her. My 80-year-old aunt Eve set up a trust that included my sister. She would get a small sum after her death. Now, every time we speak she asks: "How's Eve?" After all these years I'm beginning to wonder who's retarded.

*

My mother was in the hospital again. She signed the DNR papers without a blink. She never complained. The doctor confided that her recovery was surprising. Her numbers were off the charts. Her chief complaint was the diapers she was forced to wear. I sat at her side, mostly in a trance, while she slept. A man sang Harry Bellafonte songs to his comatose mother in the next bed. She was in the last throes of Alzheimers, hooked up to feeding and other tubes, but he managed to caress and hold her. When he crossed the room, I saw he was on crutches and had a leg cast. We spoke. He'd been in a car accident. The family had been arguing about keeping his mother alive. The father said no. His sister said yes. He drove into a telephone pole.

*

I never knew my father was sick and dying. I remember him in bed, and then he was in a hospital room I was too young to enter. I stood where my mother said I should and waved at a window in the Hospital for Incurable Diseases. I remember a gallop of footsteps down the long hallway of our apartment. I don't recall being comforted after the funeral it was decided best for me not to attend. In school, I could not say or write my father was deceased on those forms the teacher kept in attendance books. At summer camp I said he was a film star, on location, and couldn't come up for Visitors' Day.

*

I worked for a short time as a house model at Bloomingdales. Jerry Geisinger used me for illustrations for print ads. Unlike my mother, everything impressed me. Especially prices. The more I paid the more stylish I felt. I was flattered when the top girl, a girl you'd see in *Vogue,* took a shine to me and suggested lunch. She lived in an empty apartment on East 63rd St. With tiptoe curiosity, I walked barefoot on white carpet and sat at a bistro table. There was no food in the house, so we wound up at Gino's where everyone knew her. After, we went to Barney's to pick up a piece of luggage they were holding. Salesman stood at intervals like stations of the cross. She smiled at each one and in the back picked up a red lizard case, twirled it around, smiled again as she slowly made her way out, leaving each salesman thinking the other had served her. Next day, we met at Bloomingdale's fur department. The plan was to meet her mother at Maxwell's Plum. On the elevator down, Mr. Olsen, the imposingly six-and-a-half-foot head of security, grabbed her arm. He was mad for models. She asked him to join us and we sailed out of the store, one on each arm. Her mother was a Connecticut matron who spoke in those low decibels reserved for hearing tests. When, let's call her "Ellen," rose for the restroom, a price tag dropped down from the mink draped over her chair. Nobody noticed. I shoved the tag back, and only then realized what was up her sleeve.

*

After my father died, we moved from East New York to the ground floor apartment in my grandmother's three-family house in the Winthrop section of Brooklyn. My grandmother Bertha, my father's mother, had personality to spare. It took us an hour to get down the block. Everyone stopped. She ran gin rummy games and played mostly with men. All the furniture she owned, she was proud to say, was purchased with winnings. She talked politics and sex. The first advice I got was give a little but not a lot. I became her "secretary." She didn't read English so I wrote letters to her sister in Russia who she hadn't seen in forty years. She pegged my pants. And was about to marry a third husband after a line of potential suitors sat down for interviews in her living room where I kept mental notes on each. I liked Mr. Berman but Bertha discovered he had a heart condition. She married Mr. Hirshfield which was a big mistake. But not for long because, healthy as he seemed, he died. In her final years she moved to Montreal and lived in a nursing home near her daughters. I spoke at her funeral. I liked her a lot. Afterward, a Mr. Cohen came over to me. He held out his open hand and gave me her barrettes. "I used to comb her hair," he told me. "If they'd let me go with her to the hospital she'd still be alive." Sitting shiva, a cousin told me how embarrassed Bertha made my aunts with her accent and all her boyfriends.

*

My mother joined Parents Without Partners. One Saturday night a young, nice-looking man came to our door. "You must be Roberta," he said. "You must be an idiot," I replied, and slammed the door in his face. It's a story my mother likes to rehash. It's horribly true. I didn't want anyone to take my father's place, and no one ever did. For years my mother had a friend named Mac. They met folkdancing. He had a reputation among the dancers because he knew all the steps and had his pick of women. He was nothing to look at and had one eye that kept blinking. He was also a nut who believed in Edgar Cayce's propositions. He also propositioned me. When he asked my mother to marry him, she refused. "Why should I have to take care of a crazy old man?" She lived alone most of her life and had strange ways. She was clean but sloppy. Papers collected on every surface. Bananas ripened in bowls under armchairs, bank-books were kept in the bottom of garment bags. Dustbusters that didn't work were plugged into every outlet. No one could eat in any place but the kitchen and could comb their hair only in the bathroom. After a day stuck in traffic taking her to the pain clinic where we spent six hours, my husband felt sick and exhausted. She said he couldn't lie down on her bed. It was unsanitary.

*

I took her to the doctor frequently. She got more attention because I was with her, but resented that too. When I attempt to edit her complaints for the sake of clarity, she screams, "Let me speak!" so loud it startled the receptionist. She goes over each prescription ("pisscription") so carefully to make sure no errors were made. "Hold your horses!" she protests when I attempt to put her coat on. On the way back in the car I comment on the doctor's thoroughness. "He's OK." Only when I return from the pharmacy with a sack of medications does she almost thank me. Of all the things I buy to please her, only the oddest register. I bought T-shirts from Act Up for her to wear as nighties. Her favorite was a graphic of two emblazoned white condoms kissing. She liked the cute faces. When she wore it outside, I explained the message might attract the wrong kind of attention. "So what?" she brushed me off. "I like the raglan sleeve. It makes me look thinner."

Losing Streak (1)

> "I lost my mother's watch. And look! my last, or
> next-to-last, of three loved houses went.
> The art of losing isn't hard to master."
> —Elizabeth Bishop

I'm worrying aloud about my mother again. She had a cold that's knocked her out. I requested a nurse, who found her in bed in her 100-degree room with the AC turned off. So I hired an aide, who's charging more for part-time help than the full-time I fired for barely giving my mother any time at all. Bastards, my mother would have said. "Bastards" was my mother's favorite curse word I didn't think I'd miss.

Three years ago, my mother's attending at Maimonides, a young, handsome "Dr. R," as he liked to be called because nobody could pronounce his long Russian name, took me aside to say the mass in her pancreas was likely cancer. She was too frail for surgery, he thought, re-angling his stethoscope in a mirror, considering it like an expensive tie. His starched, white collar was sharp enough to cut a cake. I called in the Director of Gerentology. She said "not necessarily" when I conveyed Dr. R's findings. She wore drab street clothes, kept her stethoscope in her pocket and didn't give my mom the hug Dr. R did. But she was right. Pancreatic cancer kills quickly. And my mother is still here.

Each time we speak over the phone, she asks: "Where are you?" Which makes sense because Brian and I live in two places. "What day is it?" Sometimes I need to think. So far, she's never asked me *who* I am. I give her an update on the garden. She says Sungolds are expensive; you could sell them for profit. She laughs her little laugh. I say they're all for her. She says she only wants one. Brian notices my voice changes when I talk to her. I sound like a child. When I report that I have a sty she goes into mother-mode, prescribing boric acid, hot compresses and patience. She may have forgotten what she had for lunch ten minutes ago, but she still remembers her remedies.

    I try not to think that at ninety-three how much time she has left. When my first dog turned ten, I became preoccupied that his old age signaled imminent death. I'd check up on him every time he closed his eyes. One day he ran off. This was a dog, exceedingly smart, who never needed a leash. I searched, advertised and put up posters. My mother was certain that a standard poodle, so good-looking and groomed, had been stolen. Many dogs were being swiped at this time. All the same, I knew exactly why he'd left, my sentient dog. He wanted to spare me the sadness of his death.

Losing Streak (2)

"You don't call for weeks at a time." I call every day, sometimes more than once. Afterward, I think: Why call every day when she thinks I haven't called at all, when I can call less and say I've called more? I cradle the phone I was afraid to pick up. I never know what mood she'll be in. No matter how I steel myself she gets me every time. I stumble over the chair. I lose my hairclip. I look on the ground. *Losing ground.* The meaning sinks in. My mother was a folkdancer, a swimmer, a walker. She insisted I walk miles with her up Eastern Parkway to the Grand Plaza Library when I was just a protesting little kid. I love to walk now and walk great distances still. But she suddenly stopped walking, her steps became uncertain. She went from tripod cane to walker, making smaller journeys, taking up less space, concentrating on the ever-shrinking ground she was losing. "I'd rather be dead," she replied *again* when my husband and I asked again if she'd like to live with us. On a sunny spring day, we were sitting on benches around the public garden of her apartment complex. All seats were occupied by old men and old women, but the atmosphere was lively. I eavesdropped. Conversations mostly compared ailments and prices at Key Food. Some faces grew familiar, I visited so often. A man in a wheelchair was greeted by the "kibbitzer" who wore plaid bermudas, black knee socks and a shirt that said MIAMI BEACH over faded palm trees. He was wearing the same outfit last time we visited. He told the same bad joke. But the man in the wheelchair laughed and the "kibbitzer" launched vigorously into another. My mother sat apart and sullen. She hated her kind. "You want me to go down and talk to those *alter kackers?* I'd rather read. Or be dead."

*

A plumber once tried to convert my mother to Christ. It took him hours to fix a small leak. His salesmanship was seductive. He liked her springy hair. She could pass for years younger. In the end, she didn't fall for it. He got the push, still making his pitch in her doorway with a mezuzah nailed to its frame. She relates this over the phone, advancing to details of her Meals on Wheels, what she ate, what she didn't, while I'm thinking that now the long-lived are not only prey for thieves but also evangelists. She ends her spiel with her peculiar one-chord laugh.

"He figured I was so old I'd jump at any life after death, even a goyish one."

*

While she remained unborn again, she did, against all odds, regenerate enough to make it out of ICU, hospital and rehab, into Harbor View, which doesn't have a view or a harbor, but Sheepshead Bay. Years ago, this sort of assisted living was called a rest or old age home. And while I can find lots wrong, mostly it's right. Meals my mother leaves half-eaten are decent. Dinner is served at five. Dessert, put out first, always waits on the table. The dining room is ornate and as spangled as a cruise ship's. A few diners are fed by aides. One of my mother's tablemates is deaf. The other spends his time collecting scraps for the cats who hang around the wrap-around terrace. Stepping back, the scene looks shot in slow-motion. Time slows to the extent that the elevator, which only has five floors to climb, takes forever to catch. Which is fine now. Let every slow day be the same slow day. As I enter, a woman with a walker greets me. My big smile is not manufactured. I'm glad to see lively Anna, to know her name, happy she's still around. She's on her way to Bingo. "Yesterday we had a singer," she tells me. "Such a voice. He belongs on the stage." *There's one leaving in ten minutes,* I don't say, smiling at a familiar punch line my husband uses on me.

 The day my mother moved in, she came straight from the hospital. She never saw her apartment again. We all ate dinner together. She sat hunched, grim, looking down, avoiding seeing us seeing her. Things got better. For both of us. I was grateful she was safe. She wasn't going to recover from old age. She made the best of it. She had made meticulous maps of where everything was she wanted me to pack up from her apartment, and even filled her room with photographs and keepsakes. I color-coordinated outfits and hung them in her closet. She always hid candy in her closet at home. So I keep a constant supply going in a shoebox. She was the first to point out how light her suite was and she never made complaining noises. She makes me take home the muffins from breakfast she saves for us. And when it's time to leave, I hug her until she pushes me away.

*

Before I could read, I always asked Why? Why did Dad get the newspaper every day? It always looked the same. And how? How did the Good Humor man buy coats for his kids, coats that cost dollars when I only gave him dimes? I seized on wrong points from an early age. Even my indulgent grandmother Bertha lost patience. She was old, and I constantly asked her if she was going to die. Finally, she came clean. "Yes, all right already. Stop noodging. I'll die, everybody dies, and you will too." She kept a red line-up of jellos for me in glass tulips on the second shelf of her refrigerator.

Roberta Swann

*

When my mother's memory got shot, decades were wiped out, experiences disowned, details dropped. Some days, I forget and launch into monologues that leave her blank. But she also forgets to be afraid. Her personality is intact, and if I don't ask questions she is still very much my mother, I sometimes think of her as a little Buddha, taking up solitude, padding herself up with nightly pieces of pie. She doesn't socialize, never did, but she's a big reader and still sharp enough to tell me that the latest Philip Roth is a little weird. She had given up TV, but enjoys WNYC and NPR. I let her take the lead. She does not crave company. Or the wider world. When her sister-in-law from Montreal visited, she interrupted my mother's lunch and was asked to wait in the lobby, where she was made to sit idling with her re-gifted box of Valentine's chocolates. It was July. Over the phone, she mimics her voice: "'What a palace! Such nice people! So many activities! You'll never be bored!' She sounded like a Mexican Hat Dance!" I'm thrilled she stood up for herself. My aunt's misbegotten visit was at her own convenience, squeezed between better places to be and other people to see. "Good for you, Mom. She's always been a bull in a china shop." My mother paused. "Which sister-in-law was she?" "The dumber one," I gleefully reply, glad the one person she never forgets is me.

And her grandson, Derek, who on sleepovers would sneak into her bed, wake her up at dawn with big hugs and kisses, begging for breakfast. He was that rare affectionate boy, and the only person my mother was ever tactile with. She loves to tell stories of Derek, who even as a toddler knew how to pull fast ones. He was such a friendly child that when she took him to the beach at Coney Island he'd disappear onto other people's blankets where she'd find him eating sandwiches. He was always hungry, always asking her to stop and buy more snacks. "I haven't any more money," she finally told him. But he pointed to the bank and with his big eyes at maximum blue said, "Grandma, we can get more there."

Derek was always preoccupied with money. When he was five, we spent Christmas at a farm in Pennsylvania. Clinically hyperactive, he immediately became absorbed in this rural atmosphere. I thought it was the beauty of the place, the home-style meals and attentive friends. But it was the money. All week, he went around rooms and barns picking up loose change, collecting coins in a red-and-green cookie tin. Daily, he'd proclaim how many "monies" he'd found. Everyone got a kick out of him. At the train station, ready to leave, our host asked Derek to return the money. "It's *mines!* It's *mines!*" he cried, tears streaming down his small face while I tried to pry the heavy box away. He wept the whole train ride home. I would tell this story occasionally for laughs. But as it comes back to me now, my embarrassment, his anguish, it makes me sad that I somehow didn't have the gumption to just write a check and let the kid keep his coins.

My mom would have. Would have said he earned it. Like the time she was caught up in a street fight. Two black kids were trading punches and almost knocked her over. "Where's my money, motherfucker?" As my mother made her way across the street, one pushed her and she fell. Spotting a $20 bill, she scooped it up and scurried home, all five feet of her. Once home, she unfolded the crumpled bill and kept it on the kitchen table for a week. When I recall these stories over the phone, there is a long silence.

"Mom, are you still there? Mom?"

"I'm still here. I just don't know what to say."

*

Roberta Swann

I phone my mother at Harbor View from our house upstate but can't reach her. This has happened before. But each time I panic. It knocks me for a loop. I imagine her alone, in trouble, in need of help nobody knows about. I imagine her dead. I call again. The line is still busy. How can it be still busy if no one calls but me? I take a short walk. It's a cold and windy July day. I come back crying. Call again. Debra, the telephone operator, sends a porter up to investigate. She leaves me hanging. I call again. Debra says the porter was too slow, so she checked herself and found my mother sitting on her bed staring at the receiver. She said the phone was broken. She was waiting for someone to come up and fix it. When I speak with my mother I tell her that was not the best solution. She is impervious to reason and sticks to her version. My heart is pounding. I hold myself in check and start another topic. I talk about the strange cold weather. Then, "Mom, I'll visit you soon." "I can't hear you." "Mom, I'll visit in a few days." "I can't hear you." "Mom, I'll visit tomorrow." She can't hear. I keep repeating the same line until it sounds like a lie.

*

About cancer. I only want to write: Once I had two breasts. Now I have one. I rarely recall the drive-by surgery I underwent. After I was diagnosed, Dr. Deborah Axelrod offered the option of performing the mastectomy as an out-patient, meaning I could skip the hospital stay and go straight home after the procedure, which I chose to do. What I didn't know was that I was the first patient to do this. I left St. Vincent's attached to a drain and drove home with my husband as if we'd been out shopping. Back in my own bed, complications set in, nausea and vomiting so severe and for so long I wanted to die. Brian made frantic phone calls. Finally, the doctor issued scripts that Brian ran to retrieve from the pharmacy, through a severe thunder storm. A mistake had been made. I'd been given the wrong post-op pain medicine. I belonged in a hospital. Outpatient mastectomies were an experiment, soon abandoned.

*

All illness is a foreign country you learn to navigate. I told myself I was cured. The cancer wouldn't have a come-back. I decided not to have reconstruction. Brian agreed. The idea of more prolonged surgeries was unpleasant for both of us. Following protocol, I phoned places that specialized in prosthetics. The word alone made me stutter. Most places on the list I was given were either out of business or wouldn't take my insurance. Finally one did. A lovely voice on the other end took my information and we made an appointment. Then she asked, "Right leg or left?" That jolted me out of my numbness. I reconstituted my resourceful self and came up with a homemade solution. I went to Victoria's Secret, bought a bunch of padded lacy bras and wore one out of the store. Two men passed. One said "Nice." The other said "Small tits." He had no idea how small.

*

My mother, at 92, is losing her memory after losing most everything else. It happened overnight. She took to her bed. I thought it was another emergency, something that happened before when a bladder infection left her nearly dead. But, she kept saying, *I'm not sick*. Then, when the picture became clearer, she wanted to know, again and again, *What happened?* I sit at her bedside and review our family history. Sometimes she forgets what I told her five minutes ago. Yet she remembers whatever was barely spoken. We talk about my dead father "You said you wished it was me who died instead." I deny it but know that it's true. Finally, she settles at: "You were only a child. You didn't know what you were saying." Her personality remains intact. When I praise her, tell her how she raised us alone, sacrificed, and rose through the ranks at the Board of Ed as an administrator of payroll, she says: "Don't go overboard. I took a lot of tests." She was always studying for another civil service exam which, when passed, raised her position and salary up a notch. I keep her mind going: Do you remember this? Do you remember that? When I mention her last apartment, she goes back fifty years to her "long dark hallway." Time has collapsed for her. When I phone she asks why I haven't, and when I visit she forgets I was there. We drive five hours from our country house because I can't bear her loss. I think this time I'll make her understand she's not alone. I bring photos of us together, adding to those around her room. The aide I've hired is impressing us with all she's done. My mother says she's hardly there. Somewhere in the middle something is true. Sometimes she startles me with business-like perceptions. "Without a family presence they're taking you for a ride." She wonders what happened to all her possessions. She asks if she has the money to pay for this. I sit down and stroke her leg. "Stop petting me like a puppy." I stop. That's my mother. We spend a long emotional afternoon. I cry as I strain my voice telling her stories. She listens attentively. "Do you remember," I say, "how angry you were with me on the phone?" She nods. "Why, mom? Why are you always so angry with me?" "I don't know," she whispers. "I'm an irritable person."

*

I hired Svetlana to provide extra care. At Harbor View there are three Svetlanas. My mother's was "Little Lana," a small blonde who seemed nice enough and who went into lengthy details describing her duties. "I choose from the closet what to wear. I know she has very good daughter because her clothes are very nice. But she is picky, so this take much time." In a few days Lana is more familiar with my mother than I am. "I feed her breakfast. I ask does she want on her classical music. She says no. So I read to her from book and she explains what words mean that I don't know. She is very smart...."

*

My mother had lived at Harbor View for a year and a half before she slipped into this second level of care. In those carefree days when she hobbled on a walker to the terrace we'd settle into hours of cynical insider observations about how unassisted assisted living really was. Basically, it's a business. Every extra costs. The "aides" wheel their "ladies" around like new moms in a playground, comparing notes. What they say is secret unless you understand Russian. My mom's biggest fear was that she'd need one. In retrospect, those afternoons were serene. I chose Harbor View because it had a view of the water. And something about the seagulls we seldom saw relaxed us.

*

Over the years my mother drove me mad. She'd repeat her stories a million times and never fully understood mine. The strange thing was no matter how outlandish her remarks, often they came true. In other words, my mother was always sometimes right. We were upstate for the weekend. I phoned her multiple times. She insisted Lana never showed up, that she dressed herself and took herself down to the dining room, sat in the shade on the terrace, took the elevator up to her room or "suite" as described in the brochure. For all her exasperations, my mother never lied, never exaggerated, never made things up. So I believed her. And when I phoned the director on Monday, she said Lana, "my best aide, especially selected for your mother," assured her she was on duty and repeated her eye-glazing car salesman list of services rendered. My husband was convinced my mother's memory had dropped another notch. But I wanted to believe her. I kept hearing her telephone words echo: "They're pulling the wool over your eyes.... Without a family presence they can do or say anything." The director, both sympathetic and cagey, had said: "I've been in this business forty years and have seen it a million times. They want attention. She's pulling your guts out. Stay on vacation. She's in good hands."

*

My mother's mind comes and goes, like a cat that jumps onto your lap out of nowhere and just as suddenly jumps off. So I try to bring my mother back with stories. After my daughter Nicole was born my mother stayed with me. We both heard her cry at the same time and rose together to feed and change her in the middle of the night and never got back to bed. We sat on the couch, the baby between us, and just watched her sleep. A red neon light from a bodega flashed on and off, illuminating every detail of the baby's five-day-old being, down to the tiny puffs of talc I saw rise every time she breathed.

*

Brian has been with me every step of the way, making one sacrifice after another. His feelings toward my mother have always been ambiguous. Often, he doesn't like her. While I forgive and forget, he doesn't. He lives with my ups and downs he blames her for. If you asked him what he does, he'd say: I do the driving. No small feat considering twelve years of interborough trips to medical facilities. Still, every time he yawns I resent him. "Was that necessary in front of my mother?

She already knows you're bored. Can't you be charming? You've already done the hard part." Worst of all, scanning his severe profile in the car, not allowing for the bumper to bumper traffic on the Belt Parkway, I insist: "Can't you just enjoy the fact that we're together?" Sometimes we just take stock of the visit. Other times we fight. But as my anxieties fizzle, I know he's tired. He's been teaching all morning. I feel horrible that I've put him though another ordeal. I worry that bearing witness to my mother's decline is aging both of us prematurely. He drops me off in Soho to reconstitute. I dip into a few shops. He'll recover in front of the news or televised soccer. I'll bring home food from Dean & Deluca, forgetting what I've bought because I still feel dazed. But soon the comfort of home, feeling safe and together, will bring us back to our stronger, better selves.

*

I phone my mother at 6:15 every evening when we're in the country. In her new state of semi-memory she is increasingly happy to hear from me. Her voice is sweet. She is receptive to everything I say. But this isn't always the case. Tonight, when I ask "How do you feel?" she doesn't answer "How should I feel?" She says, "Pretty good." Every time we speak I remind her of something she was happy about. Tonight, I retell her that a book of my poems was accepted for publication. "How wonderful," she says in the same lovely voice the first time I told her, six months ago. "What's the name of it?" For a minute I forget. I have a moment of panic before I remember. "Everything Happens Suddenly," I say. "That's a good title," she ventures. "It's from the first poem in the book whose second line is 'no matter how long it takes'," I add. Brian takes the phone. They talk about the chard he's cooking for dinner. "It's a taste you have to get used to," she says, and they have a laugh. That laugh means I'll be able to eat dinner tonight and approach the evening routine with a lighter heart.

*

I bruised my foot. How bad could that be? But suddenly I can't walk. If I can't walk I can't run to the stores for supplies, keep appointments or any semblance of my good foot life. For a few days there is some comfort in the convalescent world. My husband is a good doctor. He was an athlete and knows about such injuries. He measures the swelling, comparing one foot with the other. He makes me use the heating pad. And each day brings a little more ease. Still, I can't *really* walk without pre-thinking each step. Will I ever walk again? And if so, will it be with those orthopedic shoes with big toe boxes?

*

A month after my mother lost her memory she found it again. I'm visiting, sitting with her on the terrace talking about the past she can now provide details for. Today she remembers the house she forgot upstate, picking blueberries, taking hikes, falling into a ditch, breaking her wrist. The snag is she doesn't know it's *our* house. After weeks of indecision and anguish—should we consider another level of care, see specialists, put her on medication—today is a gift. Even the weather, so hot and humid in the city, is breezy and cooler here. Lana, my mother's aide, brings out tea and cookies. My mother prefers pretzels. *Since when?* Lana nods knowingly and comes back with kitchen plunder. "A bag for room." Then she slips me her bill. I turn it over and over in my hands. I open it and find it excessive. My mother is annoyed. "She doesn't do much. She brings in breakfast and disappears for the rest of the day."

*

At Harbor View aides work independently, juggling as many clients as they can. My mother, who made up payrolls at the Board of Ed for 40 years, clues me in: 3 clients at $700 a day times seven days a week equals 14,700 tax-free dollars. "Lana thinks you're a pushover." I stew. Still, whatever little Lana does seems essential, even if she only goes through the motions of care. I call her over for a private word, leaving Brian to entertain my mother. We sit under a phony palm umbrella. I question the charges. Lana repeats how she dresses, bathes, feeds, rubs her back, and is generally nice to my mother, then leans in for the finale. "I like her very much. She is a smart lady. I read her and she tells me what mean words I don't know." I remove my sunglasses, look her in the eye, and ask what she can do for less. It seems the same thing. My mother smiles when I tell her how I cut Lana's bill. Before I selected Harbor View, I vetted twenty other elder care facilities, knowing we were at their mercy. As my mother says, motioning to a newcomer with dementia in a wheelchair, "Who's going to tell?" Maybe Rose, who I welcomed over. Rose is a tall, slim, elderly woman with a dramatic manner who was a concert pianist. She lives at Harbor View as if it was Paris, wearing high heels and make-up, taking turns around the terrace each day with a walker, stopping to chat with one and all. At first she is charming, then the more she makes of herself the less she seems. "I played for Barishnekov. Do you know him, Eva?" My mother looks away. Rose taps out notes on her leg as I watch purple veins jump through her hand. "How do you like living here, Rose?" I ask. She tosses her head. "I've been here five years and I hate it more each day." When she finally takes her leave I apologize to my mother who is clearly annoyed at the matchmaking I was up to. "I thought you'd have similar enthusiasms. She's a musician. You love music." I make excuses. My mother rolls her eyes. Her face twitches more these days. "She's a *meshugannuh*." Brian laughs. We go back to our visit. And she tells me a story I hadn't heard. Her mother, who nearly succumbed to the 1918 flu pandemic, lived the rest of her days with a chronic cough she feared was contagious. "She never hugged or kissed me when I was a small child, but I knew from her actions that she loved me." I know my mother is telling me this to explain her own lack of physical affection toward me. I am grateful for the information. I tell her it's important to say things. She says it is sometimes better to say nothing "You can never take words back." She is referring to my words at age 12, after my dad died, when I said I wished she's died instead. The memory of those words conjures up the moment when they were true. She has to go to the bathroom and I try to talk her into taking her wheelchair. She protests. "I don't feel like myself when I'm pushed around." The slow traffic to the lobby unnerves me. A bingo game is always in session. In the restrooms, an old man waits to be lifted off the toilet. I catch a glimpse when his aide finally comes back. He's smiling and looks not pitiful or feeble but obedient and cheerful. "I always sit too long," he announces. I ponder his words and watch the aide, who should not have allowed him to sit so long, lift him roughly by the armpits into his wheelchair.

*

We journey back to my mother's room and pass the only married couple who live at Harbor View. They are always neatly dressed and engrossed in each other's conversation. The wife leans into her husband's ear. "No more cookies," I hear her say. The windows are open and a breeze comes in. We chose this suite because of the view. Brian points out a windsurfer and a yacht passing by. Suddenly, she is standing on tippy-toes, looking out the window, joining in. She's happy for a moment. She tells Brian he needs a haircut. He tells her she looks like Albert Einstein with her crazy white hair all over the place.

*

On the car trip home I'm elated. I can't believe her recovery, The next day I phone and we have a conversation that lasts over an hour. "So when am I going to see you—" she starts, then stops herself. "I know. You were here just yesterday."

For some time I've suspected Lana of stealing. Now my mother's good Omega watch has gone missing. My anger is radiant. She made me believe my mother was in good hands, not sticky fingers. "I rub back, give shower, fix hair, take her to terrace," she'd assure me daily in the same expansive order. When I asked my mother if the backrub helped, she'd answer "What backrub?" I was left thinking her memory was not just frayed, but shot. Lana kept us confused. She pegged me for a pushover, visits-once-a-week-brings-flowers-and-chocolates type. She thrived on the senility of her charges. When we visited, she served tea, and worked the room like a fundraiser. She cared for several "clients" simultaneously. It was only when she billed me for days she was off duty that I began to catch on. Her English was fractured, but her math was advanced. Of course, I fired her. But the Lana-loop keeps playing in my head. I want revenge or *some* satisfaction. I want to report her. Is she even registered or licensed? My husband says I'm investing too much emotion in this. He's afraid she'll send the Russian mafia our way, or, worse, I'll complain my mother out of Harbor View and they'll blacklist her from every elder care facility in Brooklyn and the five boroughs, and she'll have to live with us. Stealing from the elderly is an old story. I'm fighting a losing battle. My friend's father put an aide in his will. He thought he was signing a pharmacy receipt for Ben Gay.

Roberta Swann

*

My mother wishes me a robust Happy New Year. She enjoyed the Rosh Hashanah services. The rabbi was wonderful and the cantor had such a voice. Being a Jew is her strongest tie to life. I, on the other hand, am a temperamental rather than a practicing Jew. Still, I haven't missed Yizkor since my father died. When I was twelve I started saying Kaddish. Kaddish is traditionally said each day for a year by the eldest son. But I was all my father had. A minyan of ten old men reluctantly instructed me. I wanted to say it whatever it was. Each day I'd stash my school books in a back row and enter the sanctuary. Each day I'd say the prayer a little better. This lasted for three months until my mother was persuaded to pay someone to finish out the year. I just turned thirteen. I continued to communicate with my father by means of a Japanese music box he once gave me. I asked him a question and wound the key. A song began and the geisha danced around. Should I go steady? If the geisha stopped in front, the answer was yes. In back, no. Either side meant I had to decide for myself.

For the past twenty years, I've attended services at Brotherhood Synagogue in Gramercy Park. I line up every Yom Kippur with a thousand others to attend the Yizkor community service, Each year I cry less. But there is one prayer that gets me every time, a call and response that repeats the refrain, "I remember him." What I remember lately is a 38-year-old father dead with stomach cancer they can now cure. And a rabbi who keeps reminding us to give generously in the envelope sticking out of our Bibles. And the annoying guy beside me shaking his foot, checking out asses, who hits the jackpot when a tall, bold, not unattractive, overly-dressed widow wearing a sombrero-size hat theatrically appears. His foot stops. She is a fragrant eyeful amid the short stocky others who haven't eaten all day. "'Scuse me, 'scuse me," Marilyn Monroe whispers, squeezing her slow way past him toward an empty seat. The signals they send to each other during the prayers for the dead are discernable. Only the plump woman, whose warm thigh I've taken some comfort in, is oblivious. She weeps as I once did. It's not that I don't still grieve for my father, and for all that's slipped away. It's that the creepo next to me, suicide bombers, a stupid president, the war in Iraq and, yes, the fraudulent Lana make me want to scream, not cry.

*

The first time I came across Bernie was in the elevator en route to my mother's suite. He entered on the Terrace level with two wheelchairs that were loaded with blank old ladies pushed by hefty Russian aides conversing in their native tongue about movie stars. He greeted me immediately. *Are you new here? How do you like the place? A real Shangri-la, no?* It was good to joke, to feel the tiniest lift from the geriatric atmosphere. I gave him a smile, and exited. A few weeks later, sitting on the terrace with my mom, I spotted him. He was smaller than I remembered, maybe five feet, dressed crisply in khakis and a stiff blue blazer. My mother was prodigiously argumentative that day, and I was doing my best poorly. So I waved Bernie over and reminded him we'd met before. My mother hardly reacted when I made introductions. She hasn't the right character to take chances and distrusted his unveiled manner. She knew right away what I was up to. Still, her black mood grayed a little when Bernie, a garrulous talker with no sense of restraint, opened up. He was frustrated. Couldn't find a dance partner in the whole place. The aide he dated didn't work out. She was after his money. "I took her for a lobster dinner." My mother leaned forward. He interrupted himself to ask if I liked lobster. "Not much." "How can you not like lobster? Have shrimp. Have a steak. Have the strawberry cream pie. It's delicious!" I explained I was a big-time small eater. He gave me the once-over. He was paying zero attention to my mother so I changed topics and told him my mother used to folk dance and made her own blintzes. He nodded. "I like Jewish food. But every time I eat it, seventy-two hours later I'm hungry." My mother forced a smile. Bernie was a comedian. When he ran out of jokes, I asked him what a robust guy like him was doing at Harbor View. He said his wife died and he didn't cook. "Do you cook?" "Not much," I said. "My husband does." Brian was sitting in the shade, and allowing Bernie center stage, both of us grateful for the diversion he provided. My mother was more herself, and the day's fortunes were improving. So when Bernie reached for my hand, squinted at my engagement ring, and asked Brian if he found it in a Cracker Jack box, we exaggerated our howls. Even my mother laughed. She liked insults directed at others. But it was getting chilly and she wanted to go in. Bernie offered his blazer. I could imagine him younger as a serial seducer. He insisted we go up to his penthouse—not a joke. "Penthouse" was what Harbor View called its accommodations a price level above my mother's suite. He wouldn't take no for an answer, and I was curious to see what the extra bucks bought.

    Brian wheeled my mother. Bernie asked permission to take my arm. He squeezed. "You have muscles." He didn't. I realized then how frail he really was. One foot dragged like Ratso in *Midnight Cowboy*. I felt his inward shaking. The sunglasses, that at first passed for stylish, hid macular degeneration. Still, he was unselfconscious and compulsively cheerful. He opened his door and showed us around, particularly proud of a pair of facing double marble seats in the shower. "I need somebody to sit with." He squeezed my arm again. I felt repulsed but tamped it down. "Bernie, you're a real *tsatzkala*." His face lit up. "I love that word. I haven't heard it in years." His place was a little larger than my mother's but not much swankier. There was the same inspiring view of Sheepshead Bay my mother had three storeys down, and only one photo, his son, a psychiatrist who, Bernie said, visited once a month. "Hear that, mom?" I wanted to say. See how much better I am than that? After we said our goodbyes, we sat more cozily in my mother's suite, enlivened by Bernie's gossip about illicit affairs that go on between residents and aides. It was hard not to like Bernie, but my mother did. She called him a schmuck. I thought she would be attracted to his liveliness. She said bedbugs were lively too.

Pain

I ask Brian a question from another room. He answers me with an angry voice that startles. "Do it yourself," he growls. Later, apologizing, he confesses he was in pain. His leg again.

Pain changes things. My mother was in pain for so many years that I was too painless to understand. Now, with my yoga-induced bum shoulder that can only crank my arm up so far, I finally understand. But, too late.

She had rheumatoid arthritis. For years, we took her to a Pain Clinic where they shot her up with steroids that kept her pain-free for a few months until it didn't.

I walked in on a rough aide attempting to dress her. She was screaming: "You're killing me!" Screams so loud they sounded like a horror movie. I held her until she whimpered.

"Tell me what's wrong, Mom."

"I want to scratch everyone," she cried, and then fell asleep.

My mother had always been a quiet woman. Never one to call attention to herself. Or ask a favor. I understand now, now that it does her no good, now that she's dead, that pain makes you *mad,* in both senses of the word.

We visited her in the hospital on one of her many stays. Her hands were bandaged into boxing gloves. "Oh, Mom, what have they done to you?" I ran down the hall for the head nurse who said, "We did this for her own safety. She was scratching and hitting herself."

I sat by her bed until she was sedated. She motioned with her eyes. "I have an itch," she whispered in a hoarse voice. For once, I didn't falter. I found it first try. And watched her fall asleep.

On our country walks, she'd stop and point to a tree, or a bird. I knew she was covering up the pain. But birds were her way of not saying so.

I, on the other hand, am not that stoic. I grimace before Brian can even ask what's wrong. My mother lived alone most of her life. Only in the throes of dementia did she express herself loudly.

I wear her diamond wedding rings on my right hand. She gave them to me without fanfare.

"Are you sure?" I kept asking. She wasn't, but gave them to me anyway. She was devoted to my father. And turned down a few proposals.

While we were never in constant harmony, she never let me down. When my first marriage ended, she neither encouraged nor criticized. All my savings were in custodial accounts under the children's names. I lost everything. She helped me out.

Regrets? I have a few. But for the moment, just this: I should have worn that red-and-white pinafore made from leftover curtain material she cobbled together on her Singer sewing machine. I hated that dress. But I should have worn it more.

CHRONIC FATIGUE SYNDROME

is an unfortunate name for an unfortunate illness, an umbrella that doesn't cover the deep, shifting virus that causes extreme weakness, fevers, swollen glands, migrating muscle pains, migraines, flattening exhaustion, altered mental states and so many other neuropsychotic complaints. My moment of onset occurred twenty years ago, out of nowhere, when one morning, sitting at my desk, the room started spinning. I lost my sight for a few seconds and couldn't find a full breath. It took time to regain enough equilibrium to phone Brian who came running home. Regular life stopped. I don't mean cocktail parties or spin classes. I mean not being able to shower, dress or sometimes get up. I fought it as much as I could, imitating my healthier self, but the virus conspired against me, forcing me to leave a job I loved. This acute stage lasted eighteen months, and bouts still recur.

Which is why my feet are dangling from the exam table while Dr. F takes the cuff off my arm. I try not to notice how old he's become. Not surprising, since we've had such a long medical romance. He's frustrated because there's still no treatment, and because he's a dour guy, he does nothing to cheer me up. He leaves me alone and orders some blood work. Waiting for the nurse, I notice the cartoony Philip Guston on the wall which reminds me of a photo I have of my mother and her two sisters who bought fur coats on the same day: Muskrat for my mother. Skunk for Sally. Beaver for Jeanette. I loved my mother's fur. I burrowed my five year-old face into her arm on the crosstown bus. "Stop wiping your nose on my coat." "I'm not," I whined. But I was. My nose was always running.

Dr. F came back after two vials of blood were taken. He said I could call for test results tomorrow.

I told him my fur-coat story.

"Who's Philip Guston?" he asked.

I pointed to the wall, but he was already out the door.

I make my slow way home, thinking this is how my sister Rita must have felt all her life. She was unsteady on her small club feet, and often complained of things I couldn't relate to. Now, watching a man in a wheelchair being hoisted onto the bus, I admire his steering skills. I observe the blind woman get up and out of his way. And think of the courage it takes just to go on.

When I was first diagnosed, the only solace I took was that Keith Jarrett, Randy Newman and Cher had it too. Many doctors thought CFS was psychomatic. Insurance companies denied claims. The CDC was slow to weigh in. For comfort, I joined a support group at Beth Israel Hospital. Sufferers sat on meaty naugahyde sofas exchanging symptoms and remedies: high protein, low protein, megadoses of Vitamin C, ginseng, mushrooms, acupuncture, green-blue algae, and the latest hope—intravenous gamma globulin I wasn't game enough to try.

My mother called twice a day to find out how I was. We'd play the numbers game. Years ago, when I couldn't afford the expensive clothes I coveted, I'd claim I paid a fraction of their price. "Too much," she'd protest. *I could never lie low enough.* When she asked what kind of day I was having, I'd say a "5," which was really a "2," and she'd say "only a 5? Tomorrow I'll pray you're a 7." With Brian, I'd play the word game. I felt like linguini in boiling water. Or a dress gone through multiple markdowns. On better days I'd say I was more watercolor than oil painting. It took me a year to navigate the mean streets of Madison Avenue. Sunlight set off vertigo. At a checkout, the red scanner light caught my eye, and I fainted.

The support group was getting on my nerves. Daisy missed her daughter's wedding because she was too weak to walk down the aisle. Sue, the leader, couldn't bear *not* to hug everyone after every spoken gain or setback. It was getting hard to duck her, so I just quit.

After leaving the doctor's office, I catch a bus. I love riding NYC buses and always look out the window. I'm looking for street style that I appropriate when I write about fashion. What could I do with the man in a black baseball cap that says "Make America Great Britain Again"? I'll think of something. But what catches my eye now are the three girls in funny fun furs whose coats fill like sails as they pass. Of course, I think of my mother and her two sisters. A good omen.

Tomorrow I might just be a seven.

Rita

Her life was short. Not sweet. My sister was born with club feet. She spent the first two years in and out of Brooklyn's St. Giles Hospital in casts and steel braces. My mother dragged me along on visits, not easy, a long walk for a five year-old, but I've been a walker ever since.

She was in a crowded room with other cribs. I knuckled through the bars to fool with her curls, the only cute thing about her. She was never a baby. Or a toddler. Or a teenager. I could hear my mother in the middle of the night, crying over her future.

She wore big lumpy orthopedic shoes on her small, twisted feet. My mother watched over her, and reprimanded me for opening the refrigerator, worried Rita would catch cold. She did. Then asthma. Nibbled skin. Thick stuttery voice. Swollen ankles.

From the beginning, our lives diverged. I was as easy as she was uneasy. At Tilden High, I was voted Most Charming, which just meant not Most Pretty. My sister was stashed into CRMD classes. "Children with retarded mental development" got gold stars for everything, pasted everywhere. I peeled some off her arm. She said it tickled.

My Canadian aunts said she was short-changed, so I tried to get her right. She sat obediently on a kitchen chair for different hairdos, silent as a plant, wearing the felt poodle skirt I bought with my allowance.

She was never sad, mad or moody. I never knew what she was feeling. All my advances were artificial. But, sometimes

I loved her. At sixteen, she ran away from home and eluded the NYPD for weeks until she was discovered in a dangerous East New York tenement living with a kindly eighty year-old black man named Kelly, whose grits made her happier than we could.

What animal instincts gave her such courage? There were now rabbis, doctors and social workers in Rita's life. I was having another life as a fashion model. There was nothing to it. I kept quiet, imitating an air of secret knowledge. When the designer ran down the runway like a happy dog, I remembered not to smile.

"You're never going to take care of her," my mother said to me, without anger. So she got Rita on the rolls for subsidized living. For a while she did well, had an apartment, regular check-ups, small jobs, a little life. "She's fine," I assured my mother after every phone call. "You want her to be fine," my mother said.

I lied about my sister. She was a dancer in California, I told the doctor taking a family history. Cancer? My father died at 38. Anyone else? No. Wait. Yes. My aunt Jeanette. But as mentioned before, we weren't close.

I kept my relationship with Rita going with gifts sent through the mail. I didn't have time for her, and she didn't encourage visits. I knew her whereabouts through my mother, who got a bang out of all the Broadway shows my sister saw for free—perks for the handicapped. My sister started using a cane. I tried to talk her out of it. A cane is too identifiable. But, then, so is a Birkin bag.

Things took a bad turn. Rita vanished again. We discovered she hadn't paid rent for a year. Bonds we'd put aside for her went missing. She'd cashed them all in, gambling everything away in Atlantic City. My mother was in despair. "Stupid kid," she cried. Not so stupid, I didn't say. Maybe shrewd. I was amazed by her ability to overcome her IQ.

She was near death when we found her. She'd been living on the streets for weeks without her meds, wrecked, full of lice, running a high fever, in the middle of an asthma attack. My mother took her in and Rita lived under her protective custody for a year, fortified with good food and strict rules my sister seemed happy to abide by. I took her to movies and bought her new clothes. The more pep talks I gave, the less she said. I got nowhere. I was talking to a wall.

My mother's apartment was not the same with Rita in it. A social worker suggested a group home again and my worn-out mom finally yielded. The way the system worked was to say that Rita had no family. There could be no visits, so we kept a daily phone connection. Sometimes a deep voice answered. "That's Marie, my roommate. She has a cold," Rita explained. I was relieved she had a friend. I never once suspected anything was off. I had other things to do.

Then one day she phoned and dropped a bombshell. "I live with Ray," she stuttered. My low-functioning sister had pulled off a con that until this day makes my head spin. That she was capable of deceit somehow made her less damaged. Ray was Marie. They'd met at a dance at the group home. They ran off together and were now living in Sea Gate, a private, gated community near Coney Island, once luxurious, now a haven for Hassids and Russian mafia. I was in a state of shock. But also impressed.

I met Ray for the first time at my mother's Rosh Hoshana dinner. He was a small, skinny, courteous, cordial, good-looking Puerto Rican who addressed my mother as Mother Eva. He liked her brisket and treated Rita like a princess as she ate plate after plate. "One thing you can say about me is I have a good appetite," she said, not stuttering. He was wearing a three-piece polyester powder-blue suit. After dinner he sat and held Rita's shaky hand before taking a walk to buy cigarettes. My husband went along to stretch his legs. They came back smiling. "Ray's a catch," I said to Brian on the drive home, and watched him smile. "His schizophrenia hardly shows."

*

The first day we went to see them, I was jumpy as a mouse. It was a long drive from Manhattan. We showed our identification at the gate and followed Ray's precise directions through a maze of run-down mansions. Their address was fifty feet from the Atlantic Ocean with a lighthouse practically in their back yard. How had they scored this? Ray did odd jobs for the Russian landlord. But how odd?

We took in the vista and inhaled the sea air. They lived in the back of a ramshackle house, separate ground floor entrance, more cave than apartment, no windows, packed to the gills with mattresses and broken furniture, soiled bedding, roaches and bowls of cat food, everything in decay. When Rita told me Ray had brought home a TV or teddy-bear, she never said they came out of a dumpster.

Outside was crammed with holiday trinkets, every holiday, all at once, A mash-up of rubber mermaids, Xmas lights, stuffed animals, decapitated dolls, tiny trains, plastic flowers poking from cracked pavement—all carefully composed and maintained, at first chaotic but then also a little beautiful.

My sister sat in a crash position, low to the ground on a mattress. In the dim light it looked as if she was in a bubble-bath. I cut through the rubble. She brightened when she saw me, and because it was hard for her to stand, I fell into her lap when we embraced. I looked for somewhere to set down bags of food and gifts, but there was nowhere to put them. In a fit of determination, I unwrapped the Ralph Lauren bedding, remembering how I worried over the blue paisley print. Would it fit into their decor? And you know, it did. My mood changed from sad to giddy. She fooled me again. When I left, I kissed her hard, like Michael kissing Fredo, and hurried slowly away.

It occurs to me now that Rita might have been happy. My family pitied Rita's near-life experience. And it's impossible for me not to number her losses. But it took pluck for her to break away. And luck to find Ray who found charm in her. I wondered about their intimate life but never had the nerve to ask. I phoned once with a question for Ray but Rita said he was in the bathroom. "Are you sitting or standing?" she called. I smiled then, and still do, at her burst of originality.

I was pre-arranging my mother's funeral when another call came in. It was Ray. "Rita's dead," was all he said. She died in her sleep. Natural causes. But nothing about her life was natural, until now. I'd spoken to her the afternoon before. She had a stomach ache. Drink some ginger ale, I told her. Only the medical examiner would have known if she did.

Ray and Rita lived together in Sea Gate for ten years. Don't say it was a blessing. Just don't say that. He ran away with her ashes. I couldn't locate him, not that I tried hard. My family said I did my best. I knew I didn't. I kept my demented mother in the dark. When, six months after, she snapped out of it, and asked "Where's Rita?" I said, as Ray had said to me, "Rita's dead." And we wept together for a long time.

There was no funeral or memorial service. I have nothing material to remember her by. But yet, lately, whenever I have some unexpected good luck, I think it's Rita, keeping track of me from the grave she isn't in.

December 21, 2011

Yesterday my sister wasn't dead.
In a dream, the teacher says:
I will close my eyes, count to ten.
When they open, my silver pen
will be back on my desk.
No questions asked.

I stare out the window facing back fields.
She is not in the falling snow,
Or lovely doe, or even more likely,
The crow.

Roberta Swann

Window

"I'd rather be dead."
She'd made me swear
never to put her
in a nursing home. To be
dead you have to die,
but when you don't,
become helpless and afflicted,
where else?

A windfall
of my mother's dementia is
she thinks I visit daily.
Today she looks clean
and calm, no longer crazy
or in distress.

"Can I stay here?" she asks,
remembering her birthday, our house
upstate where she had a room,
the dill we planted just for her and
how Lana hit her on the head and ear.

My husband, staring out the window,
turns. "She was never this specific."
He believes her now. I smooth her
pink sweater, regretting I didn't take
her side, persuaded it was paranoia.
"You didn't believe me," she says.

"I did," I lie. "I do,"
and steer her by the shoulders
of her wheelchair into the dining room
where a can of Ensure
has her name on it.

Roberta Swann

More

My mother has dwindled to doll-size, so deep
into her dementia she forgets five minutes ago.
She eats in a dream like a good baby when I feed her.
I wipe each finger, feathers in my hand.

She sits crooked in her wheelchair, staring off,
dressed in a bridal-looking lacy housedress
not even hers. Her hair is scraped back into
a tight white ponytail the aide favors.

Other wheelchairs hug the terrace like wallflowers.
Sundays bring Hassidim to the nursing home.
It's 95 degrees and men dress against the weather
in mink-trimmed hats and heavy black suits.

A small boy breaks away to snoop inside my big
Katz's Deli bag. When I offer, he shakes his head
violently, alarming my mother. "Maybe he's a vegetarian,"
I joke, patting her shoulder. And suddenly she's alert.

"Like you," she says, and I'm in heaven because
she remembers something. "Not anymore. If God
didn't want us to eat animals he wouldn't have made them
out of meat," I say because she'd once laughed

at that. But she's back to absent. The boy's mother scolds, *Hak mir nit kayn chainik!* Sun bounces off her polished Farrah Fawcett summer wig. My mother used to say the same to me as a kid: *Stop getting on my nerves!*

Now she whispers "More," tugging my hand. I pull her pillow up. I think she's expressing tenderness, or maybe she wants more jokes I'm short of, but no. Now that I'm confused she's clear. "More," she says. "More," eyes on the bag.

Roberta Swann

Superstitions

My mother always made me chew a piece
of thread when she sewed on me,
(this time curtains into a dress),
"so you won't get pricked," she said
as I stood in the roaming light
of her bare bedroom where I wasn't
allowed to play.

After she finished and left, I hopped the spool
across the bedspread, skipping every
other blue satin patch, up and back,
side to side, fast and slow,
avoiding lines so God would see
I was serious and bring
my dead father back

Beckett

All but one
of her holiday gifts
arrived after she died.

They sit on the couch
next to her ashes,
going nowhere.

I wait
for the black hat
with three feathers
to arrive, thinking
next time I'll FedEx
not Parcel Post.

Roberta Swann

Jump Rope

Her room so bright
and very clean, with a wardrobe
of clothes she doesn't wear
and a big bathroom she can't use.
Floors so lustrous, yellow caution signs
are propped along corridors.

I wheel her to windows, pointing
out the ocean she swam in,
follow her gaze to balloons
stuck on the ceiling still celebrating
Nelly, now gone.

My head dips, and I hold her
in unsteady arms.
What has happened to my mother?
We end each visit with photographs
that no longer register

until suddenly she stops at one.
That's you. Me? Not me. Then who?
Who? *Who stole the cookies
from the cookie jar?*

David Blaine

Who would have thought
I had the right genes
for spoonfeeding? Here I am
teaching my mother hunger again,
getting into slow rhythms
of meat and potatoes, broken
up by ice-cream to keep her going.

But next day she's strung up
and screaming in pain morphine
doesn't stop, and gives more pain
going in. I watch IV traffic
stall and go, replacing potassium
lost when water was purged
from her lungs. I stroke her misty
hair because her hands, burrowed
in boxing gloves, are tied down.
She scratched and thrashed herself
black and blue. And that wasn't
the worst of it.

Roberta Swann

How many things can you lose?
House. Hip. Heart. Now mind.
I'm glued to rotating hospital beds
she takes less and less room on.
Small as a second. Still as a spot.
Her hand I hold is transparent.
Death is around the corner, I think,
wrongly again. She was a great one
for reductions, my mother,
a going-out-of-business sale
going on.

How crazy was I to think
dementia was a head cold
that would go away, that
a dozen new panties could cure
incontinence, that she'd put up
with a Russian aide at Harbor View
who cleaned her like a car;
who she cursed and sent to hell.

I miss the bats flying out
of her head. She's quiet now.
Doesn't speak at all. Propped
in a wheelchair, sustained by Ensure,
living in a nursing home whose
monthly rate buys a college year, down
to dentures and glasses she doesn't need.

Crack in the Door

The charge nurse is sick
of my urgent voice and constant
calls. "Your mother has nine lives.
This is her tenth." Which makes me
think of that death-defying David Blaine,
the crazy magician guy, making comebacks
from sand and ice.

Roberta Swann

A Crack in the Door

My mother was afraid of mayonnaise. She loved pineapples but couldn't cut them. She baked cakes in a frying pan on top of the stove because the oven might explode. Yet, left a widow with "two rotten kids" and no money, she managed. Taking annual civil service exams for years, she became Payroll Administrator for the New York Board of Education, putting food on the table, serving hot dinners every night, making our clothes, washing, ironing, and always cleaning. You could "eat off her floors." Not that I cared. I wanted her to wear high heels, not blue sneakers, sip wine like Sharon's mother, "the hooker upstairs," not drink Sanka. I spied on her through a crack in the door when she thought I was sleeping. She sat barefoot in a nightgown reading a book on the kitchen table. The Camel she puffed looked like a dragon blowing smoke. And the prunes stewing on the stove were for her breakfast. I could watch her turn pages for hours. I wished my father was undead even though he'd been out of work and full of cancer. To my mind, he was "afraid of nothing."

No More Sorrows

The phone rings.

"This is your limo. No rush. Come when you're ready."

He's early. So am I. I ride down with a neighbor and her dog. She's all smiles and chatter. I try not to tell her.

"I knew it was you. But, uh-uh, no dog. I'm Rudy."

The dog's not mine. I'm on my own. My mother's sole mourner. A few weeks before, my husband was hit by a truck, broke his hip and is barely mobile. For years, during her long decline, we planned her end. Part of that plan was to be together.

Suddenly, there's a downpour, unpredicted, alarming rain. He puts up an umbrella and guides me toward a big black car. I have my choice of doors and seats. We connect right away. He's an amiable six foot three Irish Catholic who loves his wife, has a second home in Florida, plays serious golf and drives part-time for the money.

He can talk about anything. And we do on the short long ride to Beth David Cemetery. Roads are flooding but Rudy is savvy. And soothing. The night before, after the four in the morning phone call, I was a goner. Now I'm talking golf and gambling, of which I know nothing.

At the gate, the rabbi slips into the car. He taps his watch. The grave diggers are out to lunch so we talk the hour away. He's full of rabbinical goo, but I like him. He says God is a jigsaw puzzle, not to be solved. Why? I think. Are pieces missing? How far can you be incorrect without being wrong?

He was in the show business before, but business wasn't good.

Roberta Swann

"Rabbis run in my family. Still, you need customers."

This could be true. Another rabbi from the nursing home called a week after her funeral, only to discover that my mother was already dead. "So sorry," he said. Maybe sorry to have missed the sale.

We discovered, this rabbi and I, that we came from the same tough Brownsville neighborhood. "Pitkin Avenue, Belmont Avenue, Saratoga Avenue ... Do you remember the Loews King?"

I do. "My best friend Zelda won Miss Brooklyn at the Loews King. I came in second!"

"I can see that."

Everyone is wearing dark, sensible suits. I'm dressed for a nice summer's day which this isn't, designer down to my underwear. The funeral director joins us. He's hale and good-looking. He gives me papers to sign, confirming my mother was cared for in the traditional Orthodox manner. I cling to the Tahara ritual washing and a Shomer who sat with her body all through the night. He hands over a seven-day memorial candle and asks me to identify her, a law I was unprepared for. He makes this request with impressive tact. We stand beside the hearse. He slides out the plain pine box and steps away. It's her, shrouded in papal cleanliness, looking like a nun at first, but very much my mother, whose cold cheek I touch goodbye.

The diggers are still at it, battling the mud I sink into. There is no path. I make my way clumsily. Rain is joined by wind. Soaked, I can hear my mother say: Who wears such stupid clothes on a nasty day? Rudy materializes with an umbrella. He takes my arm. "I don't usually do this. But no one should stand at a grave alone."

The rabbi knows his Hebrew and psalms and reads from notes he gathered from me the night before. She was widowed at 38, worked hard all her life and raised a family alone. She'll rest now beside her husband in the double plot she purchased 60 years ago. I study my father's stone until it starts to blur. The rabbi says a prayer that phrase by phrase I repeat after him. When he switches to clanking English rhyme I look at the sky.

In the distance I see coffins stacked like firewood. My mother is lowered into the ground. But her final face is, and always will be, with me. The rabbi takes a shovel. I hear dirt dropping. I take a shovel.

The rabbi points out Rebbe Schneerson's monument close by. Droves of Hassids will descend the next day to honor him. My mother would be pleased to share his blessings, and be among the many awaiting the Messiah.

I vanish inside the limo, unable to locate myself. Rudy says burial isn't for him. He just bought two shelves in a crypt. God? He should be better at it. He's looking forward to Las Vegas. "When your husband recovers, give it a try." I won't. I barely hear him. And hardly realize we're moving until the car stops short. The rabbi catches his breath. He almost forgot. Pinning a black mourning ribbon on me, which a strong gust takes the next day, he wishes me no more sorrows.

Two

About Time

It's a nice, nice day and I promise myself not to get down. I watch three turkey vultures play follow-the-leader, circling above the house. They're not bad birds, just vultures. I've come to think of the country as a place safer than the city, but maybe it's because Brian buries the dead before I wake up. The come-and-go sharpshinned hawks are here again. I'm attracted to hawks, tough guys no one messes with, majestic and well-made. But I fear for the baby robins, already stretching out of their nest, testing their flying muscles. I keep checking, but know I can't stand guard every minute. Maybe the turkeys, filing by like monks on a meditation walk, have the right idea: Just do what you do and hide in plain sight. The hummers whizz past my nose to the feeder—each year, all the way from Mexico just to get at our sugar-water. Brian's seen deer, a mother and two fawns. We watch them leap through our front woods, ears like flashlights, Brian says, exactly right, like most of his words, except when we play Scrabble, which is most nights in the country. He complains that he attracts vowels, never goes first, gets good letters, or wins. Last night I got two scrabbles and scored 460. I secretly play against my highest score. I'm good, smart and strategic. I suggest squarely to Brian that he channel a luckier version of himself and stop sitting so stormy-faced and grumbly. Despite a Cambridge Double First and a Princeton PhD he loses 90% of the time. Still, he keeps playing and keeps meticulous records of our scores, going back months.

*

You wouldn't consider a diagnosis of breast cancer lucky, but when my biopsy came back a lucky stage 1 that's what I felt, or felt that's what I should feel. Dr. A was my surgeon, respected and renowned in her field. She suggested I try a new option, an out-patient mastectomy that would allow me to go home the same day. I bowed to her reputation, convinced I was in good hands. On the day of my surgery, I waited in my paper nightie and shower-cap an hour past schedule. When she finally put in an appearance, fresh from the gym, she said she always felt better after a good workout.

*

What can I say about walking into an operating room? That it looked like a spaceship. I was a robot climbing onto a cold, metal table, handing over an arm, strung up to an IV, swabbed and stenciled without a word of protest, thinking this could not be me. I'm not this brave. I'm more the hysterical and raging type. But there I was, scared but stoic, leaving my husband behind in the small waiting room, hoping he'd be OK, because despite the fact that my breast would soon be medical waste, I'd be OK.

"You're fine. The procedure went well," someone said after I woke. I was given pills to repel pain. Maybe I fell asleep. Brian came in. Somehow I got dressed, after noticing my chest was neatly bandaged like it was run over with a tape dispenser. A drain hung at my side like a handbag. I waited in the lobby of St. Vincent's, dazed and numb, until Brian brought the car around. It felt weird, like leaving the scene of a crime. Weirder still, to be back home, riding the elevator with an oblivious neighbor and answering "well" to her "how are you?" Everything changed the minute I got into bed. I was seized with nausea and vertigo so bad I couldn't breathe. It took an hour for a doctor to get a script for Compazine to an inconvenient pharmacy that Brian had to run through a lightning storm to collect. Later I learned that out-patient mastectomies were experimental, that I was the first to consent, and that they'd been discontinued. I was lucky to come through as well as I did and, like so many before me, survive.

*

The day we took the car in for a new radiator there was a flood watch for Delaware County. We killed two hours at Fairview Library in Margaretville. An accomodating librarian informed two other patrons that their cars were ready. Years before, the town was underwater, and it took the National Guard and federal funds to restore it. There was real concern as rains came down hard. When we'd moved up, shops on Main Street displayed water-level marks high as four feet. Reconstruction was so successful a few movies were subsequently shot using Margaretville as bucolic small-town backdrop.

We arrived home with an unexpected feeling of well-being. The car was fixed. The electricity back on after another frequent power failure. We were safe from the storm. Over the phone, my mother remembered that the noisy coffee I used to make was called cappucino. Small triumphs toward better days. I unpacked groceries I'd bought at the A & P. Whenever I shop I buy doubles. In the country for the city. In the city for the country. I took peanut butter and pasta down to the mudroom to include in the bag already filled with an assortment of things earmarked for the city. *It wasn't there.* In a flash, I somehow knew Brian had mistaken it for trash and scooped it up with the other garbage bags we'd just taken to the Transfer Station en route to the garage. Dread invaded me. Then panic and mounting alarm. In that bag I'd hidden Brian's birthday gift, a vintage Rolex, for surprise and safe-keeping, planning to personalize it at the local jeweler's. My head was spinning. At first, Brian was doubtful, but after backtracking his moves he knew he'd made the blunder. Still, he thought my panic out of proportion, that we'd only lost a few bags of provisions. I said my good luck Gucci silver bracelet was inside to camouflage the real truth and give myself permission to feel as sick as I did. I was certain the bag was gone, but still kept searching house and car. The Transfer Station was closed by now and closed the next day. I left messages there, and at the Town Hall, hoping someone could exercise authority. But no one found a minute to call us back. This was no ordinary muddle to minimize. This was a Rolex Brian didn't even know was missing. He never liked expensive watches. And now he didn't have one.

*

After my divorce, none of my material losses registered. Brian gave up his bohemian digs in the West Village and we moved across town, renting an apartment with two bedrooms. We'd met at the 92nd St. Y, where he was teaching a poetry workshop. I'd written two poems. Despite the legal chaos and custody disputes, I battled through; we settled in. I felt comfortable. Our friends were mostly writers. One afternoon I came home to find Brian and Seamus Heaney sitting cross-legged on our living-room floor discussing ancient Irish bog burials. I had nothing to add, so just offered tea. Later, I looked at the books Seamus signed that day. In *Wintering Out* he wrote, "Brian, 'the end of art is peace,' Seamus, on the eve of the 80s, 31 December, 1979," and in *North,* "Brian, 'we men of the north/ had words to say', Seamus, 31 December, 1979."

*

Long ago, a few months after we had met, Brian left on a long-planned sabbatical to Europe. I felt lost without him, and when he phoned from Rome asking me to join him, I did. His poem, "Piazza S. Egidio, 9," published in *The New Yorker,* marked that moment and changed our lives forever. I was jumping-up-and-down happy, so full of self-confidence, fearless. I had a few weeks to get ready, get a passport, plane tickets and a root canal. Outfits spread over chairs and sofas. Editing my makeup bag became as important as finding a real-estate agent to sell my house. Concision was important. We were staying abroad a year, traveling from Italy to Greece and Turkey. I stuffed panties into shoes, jewelry into socks and didn't underestimate the value of pretty clothes. I took what I loved and gave the rest away. I'd been working as a model, accumulating quite a wardrobe; my friends had a field day. Finally, the night before take-off, I put two new and neatly packed suitcases by the door, a vision of new beginnings. I was as enthusiastic about throwing things away as I was about packing. I used to collect owls, but had just read they were symbols of death. So out they went, gathered in a big cardboard box, sitting alongside brimming cans of garbage for the sanitation men to haul away. What I discovered too late was that I'd hidden $3000 inside the hollow silver Cubist owl that split in two, all the money I had in the world. I have scant memory of how I managed not only to cope but to conceal my blunder. My mother gave me the money I needed, no questions asked. I never told Brian. Or anyone else.

*

Brian rationalizes that rain and closed roads mean if he arrives first thing Friday morning there's a chance he can get our bag back. He remembers where it landed, the green and brown Whole Foods paper bag. I, a magic thinker, think so too, and see all the white plastic sacks with red twisties, so bad for the environment people shouldn't still me using them, and my paper one floating on top, bobbing on the surface, so easy to pluck, a happy ending to our turmoil, something amusing to tell our friends when the conversation turns to stupid things.

By force of will, we spend electromagnetic-storm Thursday cleaning house, maniacally banging in loose nails, gluing down a flap of curling wallpaper and repairing a metal window-frame, keeping hopes and fears on the periphery. It's still raining. We look out over the raised garden, praising Brian's drainage ditches that send rain pouring away instead of pooling or washing off the soil. We admire and take comfort in our mother robin who protects her nest, sitting beside her chicks in the storm. I re-read a Zen book, not convinced I can practice non-attachment when a Rolex is involved. I try not to think we've been more than a little unlucky lately. I know things happen, good and bad, for no reason, beyond explanation. Most of all I try not to reproach Brian, who didn't diminish or deny the mistake he couldn't imagine making.

*

Back to work, I plunge a brush down the toilet, displacing water, and see a sci-fi movie scene, a wide and spectral shot of landfill the camera slowly pans, then stops for a close-up of a great big dump-truck, strung with lights, releasing an avalanche of garbage, with my green and brown bag dissolving into blank nothingness. I can't figure out if this is a good or bad omen.

Friday comes. Brian's been up since dawn, waiting to take the drive to the Transfer Station. He tucks me back into bed. I listen to the car back down the long drive. I feel uneasy. Why did I make such a fuss? I should have sucked it up, thought of the loss as a charitable contribution to the universe. Good things happen on Fridays. Then Friday the thirteenth pops into my head. I turn on the bedside radio that doesn't get the one station it usually gets. Forget that. Maybe by chance or grace Brian will come back bearing good news. But he's back, unexpectedly soon. "No go," he says. "The trash is picked up daily. Your bag is gone." He looks bewildered and makes a hopeless gesture. I notice he's wearing his heavy work boots. "I was prepared to jump into the pit." Knowing Brian as well as I do, never one to sentimentalize or use fake words, I believe him. And it breaks my heart.

Epilogue:

Time heals? I no longer feel the loss of money or watches. But the loss of people somehow grows larger. Another loss I seldom let surface is my daughter, Nicole. Lost in a divorce. Not physically. But over the years, she's evaporated, becoming more self-righteous, unforgiving, and self-indulgent. Every now and again, we'd give it another go. The last, when she became engaged. I'd arranged a table at the Carlyle where Bobby Short was headlining. He'd been a guest artist with the American Jazz Orchestra, and we'd become friendly during rehearsals. He was happy to dedicate some songs to Andrew and Nicole. I knew she'd be impressed with the attention and celebrity. Brian and I prepared a 7 p.m. dinner with care, giving us enough time to catch the 10 p.m. show. We waited and waited. Left message after message. At nine, Nicole phoned. When I asked, calmly as I could, where she was, she said "New Jersey." Our date? "Was it definite?" was all she said. No apologies, excuses, regrets. Brian and I dismantled dinner and went to bed. Time has not made this easier to absorb. Whatever revenge Nicole

Roberta Swann

wanted, she got. What she didn't get was Bobby Short's best wishes on her marriage that would not last.

Goodland

The only club I ever joined was Goodland Country Club, a nudist colony located in Hackettstown, New Jersey, but well off the beaten path. I'd been coerced by my then-husband who, upon reflection, had motives other than sunshine and healthy living. I could think of nothing I'd rather have done less, except repeat the Outward Bound-type cross-country camping trip we'd taken the summer before. However much I protested, I was easy to bully.

After driving through the admission gates and parking, he stripped and bolted, leaving me in the car, hypnotically watching naked people play tennis. It was the heat that finally persuaded me out of my clothes. At first, I left my underwear on, which made me look more naked, and practised walking around the snack and soda machines. Then I built up enough courage to shed everything and make my way down the long footpath flanked by nudists draped on lawnchairs, gawking at my bikini lines. "Cottontail," I heard someone call, which I later learned was the hallmark of a newcomer. I jumped into the swimming pool for cover, so all that was left to see of me was quivers of chlorinated water. I surfaced to applause. A small crowd had gathered. I had an instant conversion experience: first came the invigoration of cold water on hot skin, and then the realization that I loved being naked.

Goodland was a pleasant place, with enough grass and trees to feel like nature. It had the amenities of any rustic resort: tennis courts, volleyball, basketball, shuffleboard, billiards, swimming and saunas, all enjoyed without the burden of clothing. There were cabins to rent still blinking with Xmas lights and TVs that took coins. Most people stayed at Ramada and Holiday Inns. Bathrooms were communal. Showers were outdoors. There were restraints. Rules were posted. No alcohol, obscene language, or babies without diapers in the pool. Nudists came in every stripe, everyday Joes to a millionaire whose limo with darkened windows I'd spotted in the parking lot. Old-timers, those who'd been coming for decades, liked to say: Naked, everyone's the same. No one can tell if you're rich or poor. They were glad to talk your ear off about that. I didn't buy into their manifesto, but got their point. My observation was that there is no genetic justice. The human body is not standard issue. I couldn't help distinguishing between the physically gifted and the wobbly behinds. Nor could you count on every friendly gesture being sincere. There were swingers. This was the seventies. I was propositioned but never pressured when I declined. There was also an evangelical contingent, longstanding members of the American Sunbathers Association (ASA), who held meetings, conventions, competitions, conferences, lectures by activists, extremists and even a few nutcases. One believed a nude world would be a world without crime. "Can you imagine robbing a bank naked?" he asked me. I could. I wasn't a nudist of principle. And neither was my favorite roly-poly Mr. Shapiro, who kept changing places around the grounds because he didn't want to miss anything. He was a nudist, by his own admission, because he was a cheapskate. Where else could you get the girls, the cardgames, the soup-and-club-sandwich special? The Catskills? Membership was $200 a season, less for families. One family spanned three generations and never missed a weekend, a group of twenty, planting their ice-chests and umbrellas in a diorama I could depend on.

    We found our place among three attractive couples, Dick

and Dolly, Judy and Kelly, Quinn and Danu, nudist junkies, mid-thirties, who knew all the ropes. You could call them pool potatoes except they took time out for competitive games of tennis. You could say sitting around all day was a marathon where nothing happened, but that wouldn't be true. Behind Ray-Bans, these couples were a lighthouse watching every wave. They called me Fanny because, they said, I had a nice one. And when Danu said my ex had nice teeth Judy clued me in: Nice teeth weren't a big compliment at a nudist camp.

I spent six summers at Goodland. It seems odd our families weren't scandalized. My then mother-in-law chalked us up as crazy kids. We were in our early twenties. "Just don't expect to see my *tuchus* there." Friends who were wild in other ways stayed clear. Nudity was not for everyone. But everyone was curious. My gynecologist couldn't help wondering about my over-all tan. I said I was a vegetarian. On Madison Avenue I once lost my wallet that I suspect was only returned because the man who found it was titillated by that bright yellow ASA card. He kept me in his office, pumping me with probing questions like: What do women do when they have their period? I clipped the string off my Tampax, I didn't tell him. He was a jerk, just the type you'd want to keep his trench coat on.

I met a few men I wouldn't have met anywhere else, including "Bond, Tony Bond," as he introduced himself. I'd noticed him before. Everyone noticed him. He had an enormous penis that Dolly dubbed a Duroflame log. I just thought he looked excessively naked. Tony was appealingly frank, the kind of tough, good-natured guy I liked. He was an electrician, a union man, who lived with his wife Marie in Howard Beach. Marie needle-pointed. She sat, brown as a berry, bouffant, heavy makeup, a gold crucifix gleaming between sizeable breasts and never got up for a swim. I continued to run into him. He said "I see you're a true blonde" I punched his shoulder, pretending to be offended. Marie kept her eye on Tony, her sewing, and me. The first time she called me over I thought I was in for it. But I wasn't, only too skinny. She gave me a cannoli. And kept me in pastries for the rest of the season. She knew I knew her Tony was the real deal. She was glad he was the only Tony at Goodland. "When I call out 'Tony!' at the Feast of San Gennaro everybody turns around," she laughed. They had no children. About his penis she said: Too much of a good thing.

NUDISTS ARE NICER was a bumper sticker I didn't put on my car like Tony did. But I liked Goodland enough to bring my toddlers. Derek and Nicole were a year apart and not what you'd call well-behaved. They fell head over heels over naked swimming, naked snacks, naked anything. They couldn't help but be cute and accumulated a lifetime's worth of attention, performing silly made-up songs and dopey dances. They were given so much ice cream and cookies I made up T-shirts that said: *Do Not Feed*. They chased the older kids around like paparazzi, falling over each other, after more fun and games. Tony taught Nicole to swim. Mr. Shapiro taught Derek to play poker. But when Nicole clamped her sticky little hand around a strange man's penis and said her daddy had a bigger one, I knew it was time for bathing suits. Still, embracing their exuberance was happiness itself.

*

I also brought Brian up to Goodland. It was a risk. We'd just met. Our flagship visit was a success. He couldn't imagine walking around bare-breasted women without getting an erection. But he soon discovered, like everyone else, that going naked is more liberating than erotic. He spent much of the afternoon by the pool talking to a woman in her third trimester, gaining details of her pregnancy. I ran into old friends, Fernando, who was a physician, and his wife Eva, who had a prosthetic leg, who weren't surprised I wasn't with my former husband. "He was always running around like a chicken without a head, half-stoned," Fernando shrugged. Which reminded me to share a story. When Derek was being interviewed for Hofstra Nursery School, the teacher, to ascertain his intelligence and *maturity,* leaned across her desk, took a tiny pencil sitting on her ashtray and passed it to him. "What's this?" she asked Derek who was sitting on my lap. "A joint," he chimed, without a blink. And didn't get in.

Casting back, Goodland was an experience I'm glad I had. Would I go now? No. Circumstances change. And so do fannies. Age has you at a disadvantage, which makes me admire all those nudists in their grandparent years who showed up. It wasn't a Garden of Eden or a Temple of Sin. I never got sunbather's fatigue. I was beginning to accept my impulse to break rules and contain contradictions, like sitting at the bar of the Outside Inn, served a clock of clams I didn't particularly like to eat but liked the idea of. Or realizing getting dressed was the sexiest part of the day, like a reverse strip-tease. I admired the effort the women put into their clothes, Judy in her wonderful prim white lacy dresses, Dolly in fishnet stockings and a sky-high leather mini, Danu in six-inch red platform alligator boots she called her fuck-me shoes, "because she couldn't run even if she tried"—which sounded better in the French she expressed herself in. And when I discovered that Judy and Quinn were carrying on a secret affair I was disappointed. When I discovered that my ex had lied and cheated, I left him.

There was a comedian on SNL named Father Sarducci. He made me laugh and told the truth. He had this bit about the Five-Minute University, like, for example, why take so many classes in Spanish when all you'll ever remember is *como esta usted?* It's like Goodland. When I get down to it, all I really remember is Mr. Shapiro, Tony and Marie.

*

Brian and I were not married at that time. We married three years after we met, on a Valentine's day in Woodstock, officiated by a local JP. There was a blizzard. All roads were closed. So our wedding party was small, but lovely. Ray Brown, our best friend, was our best man. We stayed at his house. Brian's mother, Lilyan, kept asking for photos I re-sent three times, thinking something must be up with the British postal service. But what confused her were the photos—Brian and me and a bunch of friends bundled up in ski clothes, playing in the snow when she expected a bride in a confectionary dress. It would have been worse had we married naked at Goodland, like Mr. Shapiro, who did, when he finally met his match.

The Day the Yoga Died

After a month-long virus, still slightly frail, I challenged my immune system and took a yoga class. It gradually felt good being on the mat again. The teacher was serious and sweet and my body responded, sinking deeper into familiar postures.

I was in Cobra when I felt a tap on my back. "You have a phone call," a woman whispered. "Follow me." I trailed her to a room where a man flashed a shield, said he was a detective and had surveillance of "me" stealing a bag on December 10. Today was March 3. Did I remember?

I was in that studio once before. I remembered that. Everything went blank, including my personality which, if still intact, would have manifested outrage. "Confess and you'll be home for dinner. Otherwise, lady, you're going to jail."

We were on the street. It was 6 p.m. in NYC when anything can happen two steps away. It was happening to me, charged with a crime I didn't commit. The detective called for a squad car which came in ten minutes. During this time, he kept threatening me with jail. I stood numb and mute. Two female officers drove me to the 6th Precinct where I was handcuffed to a bench in a room where a homeless black man sat in a cell. "You got a smoke?" he asked. I didn't. I had nothing. My belongings had been confiscated. It was 6:40. All I thought of was my husband, sick with worry. Only days before he'd been in the ER for twelve hours until CAT scans and bloodwork came back with a diagnosis of kidney stones. Kidney stones pass quicker than cancer. We were relieved. But he was weak and still not well. My eyes closed. I did yogic breathing. But nothing in yoga prepares you for this.

*

The room I sat in was ugly and dank, familiar in an old-timey black-and-white-TV way, something glanced over, waiting for the plot to unfold. At 7 p.m. another officer removed my shoelaces and took my scarf. "So you don't kill yourself," he said. I hadn't thought of that. He uncuffed me from the bench and recuffed my hands behind my back. He followed me up two flights and I entered a large room with four desks, a few officers, and the concrete cell I was locked in. Cops joked about perps and compared take-outs. The cell was so cold I started to shiver. I forced myself to remain alert. The detective was called Ramos. Ramos spent the next half hour gathering forms, eating, trying not too hard to find a computer that was compatible with the surveillance tape he had. I kept asking could I please call my husband, and was ignored.

I sat before a screen and saw myself reaching for a bag from the cubby, images that looked like inkblots connecting me to the crime. "That's you," he said, "sticking it under your coat." "That's my yoga bag," I explained, broken-voiced. He shook his head, smirked, and gave me a sinister look. "May I please phone my husband?" I asked. "I'll call him," he snapped, and locked me back in the cell. I heard him finally make the call.

There are no words to convey the shock and heartache I knew Brian was feeling. I felt miserable, helpless and frightened. The thing about jail that sinks in immediately is that you can't get *out*. So I looked *in*, and under the cell bench spotted three pennies. Three is my lucky number. I pocketed them and felt some dread lift. The cops were now joking about a DOA. A girl reported a stolen laptop she'd left at Starbucks. "Stupid cunt," said one of the cops.

*

I heard Brian before I saw him. And when he saw me sitting behind bars, he gasped. "Oh, Jesus." I found his hand. Its warmth would stay with me all night and the next day. Ramos took him aside and showed him the surveillance tape. I heard Brian say he couldn't make it out, couldn't follow what Ramos was saying. Ramos repeated that if I signed an affidavit I could go home, or else it's Central Booking. Brian came back to me and told me what I'd already heard. He was terrified I couldn't survive all this. But when I explained I was innocent, that I hadn't done what they were claiming, he said, "I know." With that, and three pennies, I'd survive.

I heard Brian ask repeatedly about protocol and procedure until Ramos cut him off with "It is what it is." In front of him, Ramos emptied my handbag and wrote down all the contents, none of them unusual. He held up a bit of red ribbon. "Red bendel," Brian said, "for protection." Ramos dropped it back, not knowing, not caring. He gave me a handwritten sheet to sign, sealed my Prada bag itself as evidence, and told Brian to go.

After he left, the burden of my worry lifted. *Sweetie,* I thought, *at least you know I'm safe in jail, not dead in a mugging.* I'm finally given the water I requested. I use the restroom while Ramos stands outside. This convinces me I'm functioning. After, I get mug-shot and fingerprinted by another detective. Then still another shackled and handcuffed me to the bench. At midnight, two officers came to transport me to Central Booking, along with the homeless guy who was arrested for selling single cigarettes.

*

I'm now riding in the back of a squad car through the city that never sleeps, except when it does, like now, stopping at every red light, watching the driver polish off a sub, his partner explaining how he fell hanging curtains, the reason he's limping. The car stops beside a giant crenellated garage door that cranks up loudly. I'm led through a labyrinth, not unlike those spook-rides in amusement parks. An EMS officer asks if I'm sick or on medication. Another is in charge of cereal boxes and milk. I'm locked in a holding cell until a female officer dons rubber gloves and pats me down. What I feared the gloves signified never happened. She just asked me to bend over and shake out my bra.

Soon I'm locked into a large cell with thirteen other women. Some are asleep on shredding blue mats. A few sit catatonic on benches. Four, in another corner, are laughing their heads off, sounding like a girls' night out. One calls me over. "Hey, Blondie. You don't look like no criminal." I walk over, happy for any human contact. I tell my story they ask for. "This lady was arrested for stealing her own bag." Laughter all round. I listen to their banter. One advises me to turn my diamond wedding ring around. Another begins a graphic story about her sex life. "I love the taste of lady," she says, and licks the inked shoulder of the girl next to her. A tiny Hispanic swallows drugs the search missed. She offers me a pill. The women share survival strategies. I'm touched by their companionship and almost succumb to their request to teach them yoga when, at three in the morning, the last woman is locked up.

She's something else. Six feet tall, handsome, slender, striding forward in a long fake mink, high boots, hair meticulously contrived framing striking features. She's about sixty and speaks with authority, takes the place over, helps herself to cereal and shouts at the women using the toilet to *flush*. "It stinks." Her name is Delilah. She tells us not to lick our dried-out lips or they'll crack. "Don't let no one near your stuff. Talk to cops like they your daddy. Sweet and respectful."

She tells a massive girl with an egg-beaten Afro to slick it down for court 'cause she looks too wild. She tells *me* she was in jail plenty but was never shackled. "You got the works, girl. The detective was trying to wear you down." Soon she's kicking a sleeper off a mat she claims for herself, sits down and pulls her boots off. "I resoled them for forty bucks. Bought them at Payless. You know what they say. Pay less, walk less." She rolls them up under her head and swiftly falls asleep. All my yoga couldn't relax me enough to do that.

At 7 a.m. an officer starts calling names. I discover we are going to be heard by a public defender before going to court. Everyone except me knows the drill. "You'll be sipping a latte for breakfast," Delilah assures me. But that's not the case. And when at 9:30 I realize that some people have been in jail for three days, I begin to shake. Whatever hope I had shuts down. The thirty-nine-year-old pregnant mother with nine kids says they always let her go because there's no one else to care for them. I can't stop shaking. Suddenly, one face draws me to her. She's from El Salvador and speaks in a soft lilt. She takes my shaking hand. "Be strong," she repeats. We talk. She tells me about her job she'll lose at the post office. And about her husband who's a chef at the UN. She tells me to have faith. She pronounces it "fate." Her name is Alicia.

I'm the last person to see the public defender. It is 11:30 a.m. He notes I've never been arrested, had nothing on me, and while he's not clear about the details, says I'll be released and might have a case against the city. I can barely see him through the mesh window. I tell him of Alicia's kindness. He makes a note in her file. "Just because a person is a thief doesn't mean they're not good in other ways." He promises to call my husband and let him know what's what.

Everyone is rounded up and led into a filled courtroom. I try not to think beyond the moment, me without keys or money to get home. Maybe I'm not going home. I sit among people who have been shadows on the street: drug dealers, car thieves, prostitutes, some of whom were kinder than cops. I am as frightened as I've ever been. Only the diagnosis of breast cancer comes close. One by one, cases are called. I'm detached but listening. And finally hear my name. I stand before the judge. No comb, no cosmetics to make me feel more myself. The charge is read. The public defender describes me as an upright citizen, living in the same place for thirty years, arrested in a yoga studio for taking a bag I claim is my own. I'm released. The public defender tells me to call my husband at his office. "He's waiting."

I'm dazed, relieved. But don't feel free. I take a seat in the gallery. Alicia's case comes up next. She too is released with a June 11 hearing. We embrace. She was arrested for a $17,000 credit card fraud.

When I get through to Brian we exchange few words. The words come later, non-stop, both of us unable to eat or resume normal daily routines for months. There is that up/down/sinking/flying feeling. We have no frame of reference. We don't know legal procedure or what will happen next. Post-traumatic stress disorder is the aftermath of the thing you didn't see coming.

I walk from Center Street to Cooper Union so fast I'm there in twenty minutes. When I see Brian's face, I know he's been up all night. We walk home and stay at each other's side. At the weekend, we drive up to our country place. The long ride is short. Brian starts a fire. The rooms warm. It rains one day and snows the next. Every moment together is precious. Almost too precious. We are full of heightened feeling. But still afraid.

Discounted

After my arrest on March 3 and lock-up in the Tombs overnight, I stood in Criminal Court at noon the next day and was given a D.A.T. that required me to appear on June 11. These three suspended months were unmooring. Life did not skim along as usual. I was never for one moment at my ease. While admittedly Brian and I are overwrought by nature, and perhaps disproportionally worried, there did remain the real possibility of prison. Grand Larceny is a charge that knocks the wind out of you. That this was at odds with the truth was a matter for our legal system to decide, and out of my hands. After retaining an attorney, consulting with him for half an hour, writing a $6,000 check, we never saw him again until my day in court. When someone who has no criminal past, who is unacquainted with legalities, gets bogged down with a crime she couldn't even imagine committing, it's hard to shake off fear. I couldn't watch "Law and Order" in the same way. In fact, I could not watch "Law and Order" at all. Just hearing words like "defendant," "plea bargain," "bail," "bench warrant," "felony," "indictment," "inmate," "prosecutor," caused panic. Even the word *innocent* made me anxious.

My attorney did say that having heard nothing from the DA's office was a good thing, that the evidence against me was weak. All along I'd been rallying for the opportunity to testify before a Grand Jury, certain I could prove the bag in the surveillance tape I was accused of stealing was my bag, that surely the technology exists to make the match. In retrospect, I was comically naive. I wanted to tell the woman who lost her property, I understand. I'd been the victim of two purse-snatchers, once in Bloomingdale's when a woman swiped my bag and handed it off to another woman who was already disappearing down the elevator by the time I gathered the wits to scream. I wanted to tell Detective Ramos he got the wrong woman. I wanted to thank the young Asian officer for his show of kindness, for the bottle of water he brought me, for the sympathetic look in his eye. I actually was misguided enough to truly believe I would do this.

June 11 arrived at last. And felt like an aberration, like waking early for a funeral, dressing in dark colors, gaining then losing optimism, hardly speaking for fear of re-frightening ourselves. We took the subway to City Hall and walked to 100 Center Street, using the same entrance I exited after spending the night in jail. We stood in line, walked through security, set off alarms—probably belt buckles—stood still for a frisking, and made our way to the second floor. Dan, our attorney, arrived soon after, hardly recognizable since we'd seen him so briefly three months before. The courtroom opened. A black female judge presided. I watched Dan confer with the prosecutor. And then he walked toward me.

"I have good news and bad news, but mostly good news." The charges against me were "discounted" to "disorderly conduct." I was ordered to pay court fees and given two days of community service. I turned to see the relief on Brian's face. I could feel my own anxiety lift but at the same time anger rose. I wasn't given a get-out-of-jail-free card. I was still punished for a crime I didn't commit. And while Dan explained my case would be sealed after a year, I still had a record. He explained that proving my innocence would take six more court sessions and stupendous legal fees. And while he wasn't the warmest and most empathetic guy, he was forthright. He could have milked us for much more money by prolonging the proceedings. When I stood before the judge and she asked if I was pleading guilty to a misdemeanor, all I heard was "guilty." It was Dan who prompted, "say yes."

*

Thirty years before, Bernie Fromartz was the lawyer who handled my divorce. He was a friend and neighbor who lived on Bedford Street in the Village, who folkdanced with Brian, who had us over for dinner. Bernie was warm and full of empathy. But instead of winning, he lost and landed me on page three of the *New York Post* with a panoramic photo of my two children, my ex and the dog under the banner KIDS LOVE MOM BUT WANT HER TO PAY. I became the first woman in New York to pay child support. Ex made the case that when I stopped fashion modelling to become a writer I deprived my family of higher income. He won. I lost. Bernie said: "At least you're rid of the bum." Who could argue the point?

Maybe Dan, who sat beside me now, outside the courtroom, waiting for paperwork. I joked, "You were bored. You like murder cases." He didn't disagree. "Most of my clients are not like you. They're guilty." If that was the closest I was going to get to a full pardon, I took it. When I went to sign up for community service, I felt almost giddy. "Could I teach writing to inmates or help the homeless?" I asked the woman who didn't look up from her computer. "Only cleaning," she said. "Do you want parks or subways?"

A few days later we were driving on the Belt Parkway to see my mother when the red warning light came on. We pulled the steaming car over to the side. And before we could worry what to do next, a tow truck materialized, like some great wonder. In five minutes we were hooked up and sitting high in the cabin with "Donald," driving to Tommy "Bugg" Auto Shop.

Donald was a big, strapping, red-haired young guy with a sweet, open, Scottish freckled face who told more about his personal life than I wanted to know. But under these circumstances, we were happy to hear about his ex, his girl, two kids, six-days-a-week job, the Coast Guard or maybe State Police he was considering joining if he didn't start his own towing service.

Tommy "Bugg" turned out lucky too, an old-time garage on McDonald Avenue in the Gravesend section of Brooklyn with an honest maestro-mechanic, no Coke or candy machines, just no-nonsense good service. He replaced an old leaky radiator cap and a thermostat our pricey Honda dealership never changed in our ten-year, biannual, $100 per hour service and check-ups. During our wait, the phone rang on and off. "What's up? Yeah, yeah, no, no, you want Johnny Knuckles, not Johnny Elbows." I knew the red-and-white vintage Cadillac waiting for pick-up was no movie prop. Brian and I walked round the block, keeping an eye out for a drink place. Nothing doing. No vanilla-candle-smelling soy lattes in this neighborhood still keeping it real. Only after we arrived at Harbor View at dinner instead of lunch did someone clue me in that the day was Friday the 13th.

Lucky Friday the 13th. Had the car overheated elsewhere, in heavy traffic, during the recent heatwave, we'd have been in big trouble. Money? These days, instead of sending checks to charities, I like overtipping the Donalds and Tommy Buggs, people you might never run into again but you're glad they're around. During my ordeal, I scanned all the local newspapers, searching Police Blotters for my name, unable to even fathom what shame and humiliation I'd feel if I found it. When we left the courthouse, we pushed through a crowd of reporters and photographers waiting for someone not as lucky as us, leaving them in our wake, going back into the world. But without my "stupid Prada bag," as my mother called all my bags. No matter who I called, how many times I called them, I never got my property back. I loved that bag.

Roberta Swann

Community Service

On the Sunday before the Monday of my community service, Brian and I did a dry run to relieve our apprehension. I'd imagined the New York Department of Juvenile Justice to be like a hangar or jail. We took the A train up to 145 Street. It was our first trip to Harlem. The streets were full of friendly church ladies out in numbers, dressed in big hats and shiny print dresses. One, taking in our perplexed looks, directed us across the street. The Department of Juvenile Justice was located in a three-storey house with sealed windows and no marker, except for a soiled American flag drooping over the patio. (I learned later that the Lutheran church next door leased it to the city. The facility housed up to fourteen girls who'd committed non-violent crimes. 95% were black or Hispanic). We walked around like tourists, admiring the old brownstones. New constructions were going up everywhere. On Adam Clayton Powell Boulevard we caught the M3 bus back to Union Square, all on one transfer. The hour-long trip was better than that provided by the tour buses we kept passing. If I spread the word, that everyone could go anywhere on a one-trip Metro card, I could single-handedly kill their business.

    The instructions from court-assigning community service nourished new fears: Bring gloves, wear old clothes and sneakers, do not bring bags, phones, drugs or family members. Failure to report could result in jail time. The "Mr. M" I was to report to, whom I imagined would be old, turned out to be an affable, uncommonly sweet young Hispanic man named Ben, who requested ID and signed me in. I'd decided in advance to do whatever was required well, and keep my mouth shut. Ben assured me that trading stories was the norm. He himself had spent time in jail, falsely accused. The last lady he'd assigned mops to was arrested for filling a friend's pain-killer prescription. She owned a fancy chocolate shop in Soho I knew well and frequented. Ben rattled off more stories. It struck me that each one sounded shady, that everyone who pleads innocent sounds guilty, including me.

Ben brought me a big bucket of water, a string mop and assorted cleaning supplies. He tagged along, assisting me as I scrubbed down three already spotless bathrooms, while I thumped around dustless carpets. I couldn't help commenting how tidy everything was. He shrugged sheepishly, and said that the place was overseen by a caretaker. Mostly we chatted. He didn't buy my lawyer's version of a sealed record. "Just commit a crime, and see how fast your mug shot pops up." I'd forgotten about my mug shot, hadn't in all these months of exaggerated worry even thought about that blatant aspect of my arrest. Thinking of that now makes me feel I am all of those no-see, no-hear, no-speak monkeys, while deep down inside I wanted to wish everything away. Not Ben. He knew the score and the system. And when at 11 a.m. he said I was finished for the day, I didn't step away smartly. Instead, I asked the director, a steely-looking black woman, if I could teach a yoga or creative writing class my next and final day. I wanted to contribute *something* useful. What good had my flourish of mops been? Her "no" was chilly, but as Ben turned me out, punching a code into the secured door, she softened a bit and thanked me for the offer.

So Tuesday the same. Except I was joined by another community server who'd driven his BMW straight in from the Hamptons. Was it OK to park on the street? he asked

Ben. He had a gray spiky haircut and wore monogrammed shorts. This was the first of his seven days and he was more vigorous on the vacuum than I, making my work-load even lighter. Without knocking around, he set the machine on a loud growl as I sprang after him lifting scatter rugs. He completed his business with dispatch. This guy cleaned like a pro. He later let slip he owned a brownstone in Brooklyn. We both got to leave at 11 a.m., singing the praises of a boss like Ben. This was a lot better than raking leaves in Tompkins Square Park or sweeping up subways. I'm lucky in little things. Without knowing it, I'd chosen an ideal destination for doing community service. With my inside knowledge of this, and subway transfers, I was already on my way to compiling a handbook. Still, I wondered what part of the community I had served. Was cleaning toilets meant to humiliate? Not for me. Nor was there anything redeeming. My conclusion was that community service was the right concept applied in the wrong way.

 I got a glimpse of a few young girls in pink uniforms sitting blankly around the kitchen table. My first thought was of their gratitude for a safe place and good food. But one begged Ben to leave the security door open so she could run away. Everything I'd imagined happening didn't. My case wasn't dismissed. Justice wasn't delivered. And the biggest blow was that the elation I figured on feeling when this ordeal was over never happened. I just took the subway home.

 When I searched for my house keys, the card I'd enclosed with a gift I'd given Ben came into my hand. It expressed my sincere thanks and appreciation for his kindness. I placed it on my desk knowing, in retrospect, my words were too many and effusive, an outburst of emotions already exhausted. A week before, I'd phoned my jail-friend Alicia and was relieved to learn she wasn't facing serious charges. I also knew, despite our enthusiastic promises to the contrary, that we would not see each other again.

THREE

A Little Bit about the American Jazz Orchestra

It was jazz critic's Gary Giddins' idea. I'd invited him to be part of the Authors' Series. We became fast friends. Why did I have Lucas Foss and the Brooklyn Philharmonic in residence and not a jazz orchestra? Bill Lacey was Cooper's president. When he hired me, he'd asked me to jazz up the programs, so why not? I told Gary. I didn't mean to take it literally, but it seems I did.

    Lacey was the sort of president who responded to glamour and fame. He offered Gary a stipend and us $10,000 seed money to start the AJO. We'd have to raise the rest ourselves. We walked out of his penthouse office on cloud nine. It was 1985. As director of Great Hall programs I was autonomous. It was a low-tech time. Cooper Union was still the only tuition-free college in the country.

    My salary was small. But I had a great office in the Foundation Building with a bar stocked with booze and snacks left over from receptions. Hungry students and faculty were always dropping in. The Great Hall had a tiny budget, but I was able to get an amazing array of guests. Off the top of my head: Tony Bennett, Kurt Vonnegut, Allen Ginsberg, Dizzy Gillespie, Isaac Asimov, Jules Feiffer, Bernard Malamud, Ernesto Cardenal, Laurie Anderson, Harold Brodky, Umberto Eco, Gunther Schuller, Bobby Short, David Eisenhower, Judith Molina, Robert Motherwell, Robert Rauschenberg, E.L. Doctorow, William S. Merwin, Russell Banks, Philip Glass, Milton Glaser, Peter Matthiessen, John Cage, Merce

Roberta Swann

Cunningham, Martha Graham, Ornette Coleman, Norman Mailer, Eric Bogosian, Larry Rivers, Martha Graham, Oliver Sacks, Louise Nevelson, Bill Clinton, mayors Ed Koch and David Dinkins, the Queen of Sweden and so many many others. How? I name dropped, pointing out that Abraham Lincoln made his "Right Makes Right" speech in the Great Hall in 1860. Beat that! So I thought nothing of picking up the phone and extending an invitation. Sometimes I made a mistake. When an emerging Whoopi Goldberg's agent suggested an evening, Brian and I went to see her one-woman show. She was good, I thought, but not good enough.

I remember many funny and poignant moments. But none more than this: William S. Merwin was teaching in Cooper's humanities department and had recently won the Pulitzer Prize. He gave a reading to a packed house in the Great Hall. Afterward, a long line stood with books to be autographed. Toward the end there was an old woman who waited her turn patiently, empty-handed. Finally, face to face, she asked, "Mr. Merwin, were those real poems or did you make them up?"

John Lewis

was the brass ring when we put the AJO together in 1985. But why would John Lewis, the revered music director and pianist for the Modern Jazz Quarter take us on? Because his sister, Marilyn Gore, was Dean of Students at Cooper Union, and Marilyn, my friend and colleague, put in a good word. Later, I learned that John always wanted a jazz orchestra that would command the same respect as a classical one. Our good luck never escaped us in the ten years we managed to keep the American Jazz Orchestra afloat. It was because of John that an orchestra creating a jazz repertory was taken seriously by Hugh Carey, the former governor of New York, who also became Chairman of the Board. He joked that he owed all of his twelve children to jazz!

Each chair was filled by an all-star player—Mel Lewis, Eddie Burt, Virgil Jones, Jimmy Knepper, Benny Powell, Bill Easley, Marvin Stam, John Faddis, Norris Turney, John Purcell, Loren Schoenberg, Bob Millikan, Britt Woodman—and we attracted special guests like Tony Bennett, Benny Carter, Dizzy Gillespie, Jimmy Heath and the Nichols brothers.

John Lewis was conductor and music director. He had a calm and gracious demeanor but was tenacious about the music. For each concert, he insisted on a week of paid rehearsals. And there I was, sitting in the empty, dark Great Hall watching it all come together, thinking nothing of it. During this time the AJO recorded tribute albums to Duke Ellington and Jimmy Lunceford. Critics called Benny Carter's "Central City Sketches" a masterpiece.

The AJO was the precursor of Jazz at Lincoln Center, which is still thriving. But keeping the AJO alive was a struggle. We went from concert to concert. Jazz fans traveled from all over the world. They would traipse into my office, one by one, to study the xeroxed seating chart and purchase tickets. That's how grass-roots we were. They thanked me for keeping the music that mattered to them alive.

I earned John's friendship with hard work. He knew my heart was in it. I was never not aware that he was an extraordinary man with a lot of talent. He never dropped his formality, but we did have some fun.

John and his family lived in a grand old building on York Avenue. His apartment was large and lived in. Nothing fancy. From time to time we'd have organizational meetings there, planning what to do next and where the money would come from. When he and Gary got into musical details that went over my head, I'd daydream. Mostly about clothes. I always wore my good-luck very high red suede heels to each concert, but I was running out of dresses. While John and Gary traded tales about Miles Davis or Charlie Parker I wondered if Bergdorf's was having a sale.

After one meeting, John escorted me out. We began to walk up the block when we ran into Anthony Quinn. Zorba was part of my young psyche. "Teach me to dance," became an emotion I measured love with. And here was Zorba giving John Lewis a big hug and me a smile. By the next block I recovered enough to ask John how he knew Anthony Quinn. "He's my neighbor," he said.

One evening, John and I were walking to the Blue Note where he was playing with the Modern Jazz Quartet. A couple stopped and asked us for directions to the Blue Note. John gave them meticulous lefts and rights. He went unrecognized while I absorbed the absurdity. Later, I scanned the club for the couple I couldn't find.

Another time, the AJO was rehearsing for an outdoor concert at Lincoln Center. It was during a summer heat-wave and John and I were sitting under a canopy of gas fumes. But something else was bothering him, something was wrong with the music. He had the horn section repeat a tune twice. He'd heard a blunder. I'd heard it too. Finally, I had something to contribute. It was an ice-cream bell. Mr. Softee was nearby.

On the night of the concert, Mr. Softee and I had a little chat. "Okay, okay, no bells," he promised. The AJO swung like crazy, even with the vagrant playing a demonic drum solo on his shopping cart.

Max Roach

gave his first solo concert in Cooper Union's Great Hall. He thought I was brilliant to suggest it, but his quartet would have blown my budget. We met again to discuss the program and I told him honestly I was no jazz scholar and he had full artistic control. "Just make it swing," I said, wanting to sound cool. But he didn't let me off.

"What do you mean?" he teased.

"Like good hair," I replied, without weighing my words, "that swings and doesn't just hang there."

And so our conversations began.

*

To backtrack: Cooper Union is a small private college, tuition-free until 2014, whose select students study art, architecture and engineering. So it wasn't every day that an art class rode their round elevator with a striking black man in a brown leather suit only a few recognized. A group followed him into my office, all smiles, and settled in. Max's nod signified consent. He liked young people, taught at UConn, and was a mentor to many emerging musicians. My office was big and friendly. I hired a lot of student help to usher and answer phones. One spirited girl took advantage of the salon atmosphere to show Max her portfolio. He was taken by a black Beethoven she'd embellished from a color-spectrum series by the graphic designer Milton Glazer, one of Cooper's alumni. This poster had become controversial among certain black musicians who took the artwork literally. Another student looked puzzled.

"So, was Beethoven black or not?" he asked.
"Only if he was also blue," Max replied, flipping the page.

*

Max never name-dropped or mentioned his MacArthur or his association with the likes of Charlie Parker and Miles Davis. And I never heard a bad word about him from anyone in the music world, from ex-girlfriends or ex-wives. (Well, maybe one). But back to the solo concert … Max played to a full house. The concert was free and open to the public. He liked that an audience who might never have had the opportunity to hear him could now. It was a blazing display, played in his mesmerizing, hard-bop style, from classics to a drum concerto. I'm no critic, and not qualified to talk technique, but for me he played like a dancer flying off the stage. I could still feel the beat hours after. Max was unlimited musically.

*

Max lived uptown on Central Park West. When he was not on the move, his place was filled with friends and rising musicians in town for gigs. There were always young players hanging around, eager to talk shop and exchange stories. Max enjoyed the buzz. He was warm and generous, When one his students needed a piano, he gave him his extra.

He left tickets for me and my husband at the box office. When they met backstage, Max immediately liked Brian because he was the author of many books, a Brit and a poet. Max liked artists and collaborated with many.

*

The last time I saw him play was at Lincoln Center. I noticed a woman I'd seen before, tall, attractive with long red hair, wearing a tight, tigerish dress from a good shop. Spotting her again made me happy. Max was the nicest sort of ladies' man.

*

In the years I knew him, Max never aged. He always looked robust, boyish, spry and death-resistant. Over two thousand people attended his funeral at Riverside Memorial Chapel. I wasn't one of them. My mother had been rushed to the hospital again from Harbor View.

*

It was much later I learned that Max spent his final time at Sunrise, an assisted-living across the street from Harbor View, my mother's assisted-living in Brooklyn. To think that we might have connected again, that I might have offered comfort, friendship, something, anything, haunts me, especially when I remember his standard invitation, "Let's have tea." And whenever we made our farewells, Max would call over his shoulder, "Stay lovely." It was his way. Maybe, in the grand scheme of things, it's fitting I remember that. And his glory days.

Playing It by Ear

At Kanye West's Yeezy concert, nobody in the eight-thousand crowd was born before 1990. It was a 19-degree February sold-out evening, with a surplus of fans clustered around Madison Square Garden hoping to score tickets. I was burrowed in multi-layers, seated beside a nice-looking black man who knew what was happening in sneakers and Supreme streetwear. Noticing me noticing him, he asked: "What are you expecting?" I misheard him say "When are you expecting?" I went blank, but recovered quickly. "What are you expecting?" he repeated, but I'd already replied "In June."

I scribbled notes during the concert. What could I say about Kanye he hadn't said himself? He was bigger than Jesus. And the Pope. But not his wife's ass, I scribbled. Did he make that bitch Taylor Swift famous? Maybe. He keeps tinkering with songs after a soft rollout so he can contradict himself. But not like Walt Whitman.

I'm aging like a kid. I have no philosophy. And, like Kanye, no rules. I enjoy my contemporaries, but in their company too long my exit feels like a jailbreak. I'm playing by ear. Out on the lam. The world is in a sorry state, so Brian and I stick close. When someone I haven't seen in ages says I haven't changed a bit, I wonder: did I look this old in high school? And when she prods: "How do you stay so young?" I reply truthfully, "I lie."

Even to doctors, until that became dicey. Now, I'm determined not to squander older age. My size remains constant. I like cute clothes. No Botox or extreme grooming.

Avoid spas and salons. Don't use products that exist for no reason. But consider Sephora the Museum of Modern Makeup. Don't tweet or facebook. Think social media stupid. But great for burglars who check for empty apartments, unless you already blogged vacation plans, and posted your newest BMW on Instagram. For the rest, it breeds envy and hate. And wastes time.

My mind spins like a wheel of fortune. But my body feels grounded. For years I practiced yoga and loved it. Now I love not doing yoga. The only way to feel good is to feel good.

I feel good. All the bad things have gone. My breast cancer. My mother's long decline. Her death. My younger sister who died a year before her. Brian's broken hip. The truck that hit him. I jumped when the phone rang, Now I don't carry one. I feel good because my husband loves and understands me, that we are long-married, and have furnished a room with the books he's published, that whenever I am alone and he is somewhere else, I feel held.

I have rituals. I plan strategically. Walking down the wrong street can make a difference. I walk fast. I choose to be lucky. Have a jar of pennies to prove it. If a number "3" on a fire truck crosses my path I'm good for the day.

My girlfriend isn't having it. Keep it real for me, she says with an eye-roll. What do you do? I moisturize with LA MER. Expensive products are better. Premium jeans evoke a feeling of fitness in me. I have many, and ten favorites in rotation. I get into an altered state when I shop. I like to shop. Mostly for food. I never come home without a sack of something good.

My self-image might be delusional. I probably look older than I feel. I'm aware that the elderly have certain collective features, so I never complain about pain or prices. Makeup is my meditation. Is it better this way or that way? Pretensions to youth are absurd. I gave away my vintage concert T-shirts, even though vintage never grows old. And those Neverfull Louis Vuittons that women tote like monkeys dragging kerosene cans—I used to be one of those women. I've repurposed mine to carry recyclables down to the bins.

My grandmother is a bright spot in my memory. She emigrated from Russia and never lost her accent. She was funny and stuck to her "gums." "You can't kill this dress. I've had it since before you were born," she'd tell her daughters, who tried to update her. She was never not a little bit beautiful. Five years after my grandfather died, she interviewed suitors. They came one by one into her living-room for inspection. I sat on the couch beside her. Her collection of china pigs, sprawled on every surface, looked as if they might run away. I liked suitor number three, but he was poor. Number five had money but also hypertension. We settled on number five who heard all about her from number one. She was a big shot, my grandmother, a catch. She owned the Brooklyn house we lived in. She played cards and bet on horses. Jack, number five, came with a plucked kosher chicken, not flowers. He made us laugh from the get-go. "I thought you'd be taller," he told her. "So did I," she beamed back. He smiled at me and tapped his cheek for a kiss. And though I was only ten, I knew this could only end well.

Recycling

Buffalo Exchange is a store on First Avenue and East 11th Street where you can buy, trade or sell your clothes for cash. Of course, your clothes must be clean, cute, trending and almost new, and you must be agreeable to accepting a fraction of their retail price. At first, I felt at sea among the crowd of kids. But I'm a noticer of things and eventually got good vibes. The buyers are friendly and don't privilege one person over another. Also, chatty and slow. So, if you're not mellow, Buffalo isn't for you.

After I offered my ID and phone number, I thumped a stack of statement sweaters on the counter. These days, I dress to distract. Then, ten of my husband's Hugo Boss shirts that he outgrew, four pairs of my shredded Rag and Bone jeans he failed to see the fashion in, a new pair of red-soled six-inch heels my broken toe couldn't tolerate, and unworn Uggs I just hated. They cleaned me out, which is rare, and, now that I'm a regular, hasn't happened since. You might say I made out like a bandit, if selling $3000 worth of clothing for $200 is your thing. Mine is recycling, so I felt philanthropic and I've been committed to Buffalo ever since.

Don't make the mistake of bringing knockoffs, which are spotted in seconds. Most bring suitcases and only lighten their bounty by a few items. "We'll pass on this," is the phrase I hear the most, as rejects are thrown back like small fish. But if you have fashion brands and collectibles, it's a gratifying exchange. The entire staff gathered round for my vintage Betsy Johnsons. And if I sold a Proenza dress that looked clerical on me for a tiny payout, so what? I spent the money at Veniero's Bakery a few stores down.

Still, my ridiculous amount of clothing is no match for this stuff-obsessed generation. On my last visit, a striking young woman sold last season's sweet things then took her gain in trade, raiding the racks for vintage deadstock, which, well, made me feel good, because *that's* going overboard.

Diversity abounds. Clothes come out of limos, shopping carts, and trash bags, from celebrities to drunks. I think recycling clothes is like reincarnation. Especially when I spotted my dress on a trannie who accessorized it with a Master Lock hanging off one ear and a studded pair of motorcycle gloves.

Bartleby Redux

This is how an unseasonably hot September Saturday in Soho plays out. Streets are more crowded than the Turkish bazaar—shoppers, tourists, girls in tight dresses ... I love New York, so join in the ballet; how gracefully we move with so little room. I duck in and out of stores, buoyed by the weight of my bags—although expensive clothing never weighs much. I cross Houston and find the Gasoline Alley Coffee Shop on Mulberry that still serves espresso in china cups. Tired now, I sit on the hospitable wooden bench outside and sink into a sort of reverie listening to a voice above me. "It's a wonderful story, Bartleby. Do you know it? About this strange chap, a scrivener, who works on Wall Street. His elderly employer is a kind man who tries to understand this listless Bartleby who replies to his every request by saying 'I prefer not to'."

I'm listening intently. "Bartleby" is my favorite story. I always wondered if Bartleby was sapped of life by his last lost job at the Dead Letter Office or was he languid from the start? The voice continues. "You must read it," the man says to his companion, who agrees. "I won't divulge more details except that Bartleby lands in the Tombs. His employer keeps visiting and providing food he refuses to eat. One day he finds him dead."

"How dreadful," mutters the companion.

"Yes," says the man, "but exquisitely realized. It's about profound alienation. It's the human condition."

I could have said it a bit better, but his voice is so soothing that when it falls silent I miss it.

"What is that wonderful scent?" one asks. "It's coming from outside," the other answers.

I turn and face the two pleasant-looking men for the first time.

"It's mine," I smile. "Santal 33 from Le Labo on Elizabeth Street."

"It's divine. Such a wonderful smell."

"I know. Strangers stop me all the time, enchanted."

I can tell both men are charmed.

"Please join us for a coffee and let's continue our conversation."

I smile, giving it a moment's thought, then say, "Thank you, but I prefer not to."

Then gather my bags and walk on, thinking for the first time that, like Bartleby, I was in the Tombs too.

Bartleby, Again

Another Sunday in Soho. A few days into autumn. Some in sweaters. Others in shorts. Cheers coming from sports bars. Couples checking out menus, floating like bees from flower to flower. Freshman crowding into Urban Outfitters to spend money they don't have on things they don't need. Homeless and can-collectors on every corner. It's that beautiful day when you're glad to be alive, despite Beckett saying he wouldn't go that far. Jokes were his jam.

On Green Street there is a two-block backup. "Go, Go!" a man in a sports car shouts through his open window to the driver in front sitting there like a zombie in a car wash. The man in a leopard-skin shirt and gold chain gets out, walks up to the window and points to the green light. I'd listen. The fool sitting in his SUV *prefers not to*. I stop, mostly to finish my cha cha matcha the barista talked me into. It's good. Two children run past to pet a big sheepdog who bites. Their mother continues texting.

The SUV still has not moved. It's been ten minutes. This is NYC. A lot can go wrong. Blasting horns count for little. I watch the man in the leopard-skin shirt walk back to his car and pull out—oh no—a gun! But it's a can of coconut water. He takes a pull and puts it back. Just then a tall young woman in a short white leather skirt, balancing two Chanel shopping bags, slides into the back seat of the SUV that finally moves, making a right on Houston. The procession of cars follows. I move on as well, happy that Bartleby is alive and well and living among us.

Holidays

We never had an ordinary holiday. In Paris we ate pizza. All the Michelins were closed. It was August. In Rome I walked miles in high heels searching for the *right* restaurant that turned out to be right next to our pensione we circled back to. On Paros, in the small village of Naoussa, we starved. Greasy Mary's was the only place to eat and it didn't open until seven. It was March. We were the only tourists. We ate with her family, crushed into a corner table. The food was terrible. But we loved it. And the jokes she told in Greek we didn't understand but laughed anyway. We were just happy to be there. On our daily walks round the island we greeted the widows with *kalisperas*. One summoned us over with a conspiring look. I thought she had secrets. My heart beat faster. She cupped my hands and poured Cheetos into them. I was illuminated for hours. We stayed until summer. On Fridays, the women of Naoussa would bring their casseroles to the baker to cook in his communal oven. Every morning, we bought our bread there. Evenings, we waited for Captain Leonardo to return, stretch a gang-plank from his fishing boat directly into his bedroom window and greet his wife who closed the shades after he was safely in. Each day, fisherman would pray for their safe return at the tiny church on the harbor, where later men would beat octopuses against the flagstone. No one goes to Greece in March. We liked that our small hotel was empty and everything was closed. We were a new couple discovering each other and this was our first trip. The locals were welcoming. Those who spoke a little English didn't understand me but seemed able to make out Brian's English accent. Dimitri took us to an unpopulated island in his outboard boat and promised to pick us up at evening. I was spooked by cows and goats who blocked the path. One goat stalked me. Wherever I went, he was already there. I was a little afraid. This wasn't a petting zoo. But Brian had a way with animals. He grew up with them. I only had a canary and two goldfish that died.

*

In Athens we were chased by wild dogs. In Istanbul, a man picked me up like a loaf of bread, attempting to carry me off, just as my mother had predicted. I screamed, alerting Brian who had been engrossed in conversation a few yards ahead. He ran to my rescue. I had to stop his pursuit. The man had a knife. This was Turkey, after all. Our friend from New York, Tosun Byrak, invited us to stay in his *yali* on the Bosphorus while he and his family were in Bodrun. Tosun was the artist who painted in pigs' blood as political protest in the sixties. He was also a champion wrestler, diplomat, and a recent convert to Islam who walked to Mecca and was now a whirling dervish. He made Brian read the Koran and contradicted any criticism of the book. I dipped in too—it was pretty bloody. His *yali* was old, traditional, and had no plumbing except a scary hole in the floor. Brian bathed me in a big, blue mixing bowl. I hardly went to the toilet. I sunbathed in the minuscule garden that at dusk was filled with the voice of a nightingale. The kitchen was overrun by mice, not the cute Cinderella ones. When I walked to the post office, the postman would only release my mail if I gave him my concho cowboy belt. On the way back from the haphazard post office, I was hosed down by workmen. When we invited our friend, the actor and playwright Nüvit Özdoğru and his American wife Dorothy over for dinner, he broke down in tears when he wandered through the house. Most *yali* had been torn down. This was his childhood. He sobered up with a bottle of wine. I don't know how, but the soufflé I made for dinner never fell. As poignant as all this was, I kept dreaming of a proper bathroom. Dreams came true when we returned to Istanbul and splurged on a suite at the Pera Palas hotel. The tub was huge. The toilet was a throne. I stayed in the tub for hours, making bubbles out of Woolite. Brian was in his own heaven across the street at a café that served yogurt drinks and borek. But things were getting dicey in Turkey. It was a time of unrest. The poet-politician Bülent Ejevit was thrown out of office in a military coup. There were riots. Fear is a good decision-maker, so we paid all we had to get two tickets back to Rome. In the Ataturk airport, two men accosted us and demanded money. I gave them all I could which wasn't enough because they chased us to the gate. In Rome we saw a TV report that showed the waiting area at the Istanbul airport where four people had been killed in a bomb blast at the very place we'd stood. The next day a purse-snatcher on a motor-scooter ripped my bag from my shoulder. Still, Rome was better than Turkey, I told our new German neighbors at Piazza San Egidio, number 9, in Trastevere. They disagreed. Their parked car had just been smashed into. There was a note of apology under the windscreen wiper and two tickets to a concert which they attended, only to return home and find their apartment had been burglarized. The carabinieri were sympathetic. "At least you weren't hurt," I said, trying to soften the blow. "Yes, very much," Gerta replied. There was a language problem. We talked anyway.

*

Our friend Masolino D'Amico eased us into civilization. He took us to a party at the Palazzo Caetani, which his girlfriend's family owned. Here I spent a stressful hour straining to make bright conversation with Alberto Moravia whose novel, *Woman of Rome*, I'd just read. He pretended not to know English and looked down my dress. I spilled wine on his white suit, not accidentally. The streets were lined with beautiful women who looked like film stars but were really hookers. I met the Pope in St. Peter's. And finally got to see Michelangelo's "Moses" who just wasn't built like a Jew. We visited Ursula and Patrick Creagh, Brian's old friends. Ursula was Frieda Lawrence's granddaughter. Patrick was a poet and Irish count. But they never had any money. They lived on many acres in a crumbling farmhouse in Radda, near Siena. Patrick grew Chianti wine. His car didn't have a floorboard. Things were always breaking down. It was wonderful and romantic. They took us to dinner. Patrick was full of stories. I couldn't believe I was in Italy, in love, with such extraordinary people. I sat next to Katya, their adorable five year-old, cream-puff-faced daughter, who spoke perfect Italian and English. Whenever the waiter passed, she'd order another dish. When the bill came, Patrick looked puzzled. "Who ordered all these clams? Who ordered all this carbonara?" It must have been Katya.

*

Brian hadn't been back to England in a long while, since his father's death. We decided we'd spend his birthday there. His mother, Lilyan, read *Woman's Day* and *Woman's Own,* and modeled herself after the Queen. His sister Sandra and her husband David had three little children who reminded me of ducklings. The pretty house in Cambridge sat on a corner lot with a garden and a gate. What was Brian complaining about? I wondered. I grew up in East New York, Brooklyn, where apartments were stacked like sandwiches. The monarchy didn't offend me. The first few days went well. But things fell apart quickly when Sandy invited us to the seaside at Clacton and we didn't go. Then Lilyan complained to her that I showered each night and she had to turn the hot water heater on. Mother and daughter finally agreed on something: That taking a hot shower every night was going overboard. It was a beautiful August day for the birthday party. Tea tables were set out on the lawn. A few elderly women neighbors gathered. One of the ducklings was playing a recorder, another a violin, and a third was sucking his thumb, gazing at the marzipan cakes—an impressionist painting in the making. Until Lilyan started complaining to me again about her son-in-law, David, who married up for money, whose parents were pig farmers in Suffolk, who was a layabout, who let the house her husband bought for them fall into ruin, who was tight with money, never gave her a hand, and who even made Sandy bicycle to the hospital to deliver her babies. Not only that. I'd heard this all before. I kind of liked David, who had ridden his bike around the world and later wrote a self-published book about it. I hoped she would let the subject drop, but she didn't. I stopped her mid-sentence. "Please Lilyan, enough," was all I said, which was enough to get her going. "And just *who* do you think you're talking to, young lady?" she exclaimed, stalking off, inflamed and insulted. The next thing we heard was the typewriter through the open bedroom window. "She's changing her will," said Brian. "Again." More was to follow. She'd told Sandy I was rude to her. Next thing I knew, the children and old ladies were scattering as Sandy shot out of the house, making a bee-line for me, lit as if she'd stuck a finger in a socket. She swung at me, screaming "Big fat cow!" repeatedly, flailing until Brian knocked her over, skirts flying, into the garden, where she landed on the prize "Peace" rose and flattened "Queen Elizabeth." She kept bellowing "Big fat cow!" and wouldn't pipe down. I wasn't fat but it hardly seemed worthwhile to correct her. David, inadequate fellow that he might have been, told her she was making a fool of herself and hauled her to her feet. He gathered the ducklings and they all set off for home on their bikes. It was all very slapstick, and funny when Brian relates it. But we left the next day and never went back.

*

Wherever we traveled, we made a sanctuary. In Rome, we rented an apartment in Trastevere. A slant of light came through the large living-room window where I'd lie down, sunning myself. Evenings, our walls flashed with the movies from the cinema across our courtyard. We found places to eat and shop and felt at home. Guilia, our local grocer, took the big red tomato from my hand and exchanged it for the small, mottled ones that would taste better. Bread, cheese and wine were purchased twice a day in small quantities. When a waiter spilled red sauce on my sweater, he sent it out to be cleaned, and presented it to me fresher than before, when we were ready to leave. That's why when my only jacket was swiped by a thug, I was shaken. I later learned that the piazza I had been seated in was monitored by the local mafia. My jacket was returned the next day in a courtly manner by a Corleone type with apologies. I was part of the neighborhood now, and they never shake down their own. Though Carlo *did* try to sell me a Cartier he didn't own.

*

Brian's oldest friend, Masolino D'Amico, distinguished author, critic, translator, made our life in Rome a holiday. He and his sister Silvia had lodged with the Swanns while they learned English in a Cambridge language school. Brian, fourteen at the time, resented their intrusion. But his mother, for once, had the right to brag about their background and social standing. They were Italian royalty whose mother, Suso Cecchi D'Amico was a famous screenwriter who collaborated on the scripts of more than 100 films, including *Bicycle Thieves, Roman Holiday,* and *Jesus of Nazareth*. She was also known for her creative contribution to the films of Luchino Visconti, including *The Leopard.* Masolini had married Benedetta, granddaughter of the renowned philosopher Benedetto Croce. She became a well-known scholar, and he became a film and drama critic, writer and translator. Silvia was Roberto Rossellini's last girlfriend, and it was she who invited us to one of his "Sundays." When he greeted me with a double cheek kiss I was speechless. Roberto Rosselini! Finally I could tell my mother something that might impress her. All this was no big deal for them. It was their everyday world. Suso was an attentive hostess. As soon as I finished one dish another appeared. She was too busy to get the phone and asked me to pick it up. It was Marcello Mastroanni.

*

I also picked up a little Italian, but could have easily gotten away with *bello* this and *bella* that because at that particular moment in time everything was truly beautiful.

*

Near Santa Fe we rented a beautiful adobe with strings of red chiles hanging from the door. We could look out our bedroom window all the way to Santa Fe. Each morning we ate breakfast on the balcony with a family of pygmy chipmunks. I picked out the nuts from our cereal box for them. A neighbor visited with two wolfhounds and a German shepherd named Bro who, at first sight, became my protector.

He was no love pest, never wagged his tail or came for treats. We just had a connection. Most days he'd visit on his own. If I was in the bathtub, he'd patrol the corridor, turning aside his gentlemanly head when he passed the open door.

We occasionally met Brian's friend Alfonso Ortiz for dinner. Alfonso, Native American scholar and McArthur Fellow, invited us to Corn Dances that featured my favorite fry-bread and adorable little boys in fox-tail kilts. He called certain Anglos he didn't like "spam neck." He liked women, especially a lesbian writer Brian introduced him to. Alfonso was sure she'd come around.

Brian and I drove a long way to Georgia O'Keefe's Ghost Ranch. It was closed. So we ate a big Mexican lunch instead. At Los Alamos I took pictures of Brian next to Fat Boy. They looked like brothers. Everything was funny. We were happy. And always hungry because we preferred to write rather than shop for food. It took things took twice as long to cook at that altitude. So we didn't.

*

In southern California's high chaparral we stayed at Dorland, a private residence turned into an artist colony. Ellen Dorland had been a concert pianist. She was 90 and flung rattlesnakes aside with her cane. The place was full of them. When she asked us to read our poems, we ran to her house fast as we could, hoping not to run into any. She said she liked my poems, but Brian's were too hard. A taxi drove us to town once a week for groceries that never lasted. By Wednesday, we were down to a block of Velveeta. Our refrigerator was outside. Inside, our house was home to deer-mice, scorpions, bats and a tarantula I learned to live with. Still, I was always looking over my shoulder, wondering what was coming next? The Plague? Floods?

*

When Leo Lionni invited us to spend the summer in Radda in Chianti he intimated that our rooms would be modest. When I pushed about plumbing he said not to worry. When we arrived, the joke was on me. The Lionnis lived in a farmhouse converted into a kingdom-sized estate on a hill, not far from our friends the Creaghs. He directed us to our "little hut" which turned out to be a villa among the oak and chestnut trees, large, airy and enchanting with a balcony to see Siena from. Nora, Leo's lovely wife, had filled it with flowers and local food. That night, from our bedroom I heard Brian smashing the walls. "What's that?" I called out. "Nothing," he replied. "Go back to sleep." I lay still, watching fireflies come through the open shutters. *Smash. Smash.* What was that boy doing? Killing scorpions, it turned out, not the mosquito or two I'd surmised.

We'd walk and drive about Chianti each day. At five we'd meet the Lionnis at their swimming pool to share our adventures. I was really excited over the *cinghialii,* wild boars the farmers feared and everyone found delicious. Brian had explained to me how they stand on each other's shoulders so they can reach the chestnuts. To me, this made lovely sense. Leo chuckled. I didn't catch their looks. I was watching Leo cutting up mouse paper for Frederick, his famous mouse, immortalized for children in *Frederick's Fables.* We attended wonderful dinners and festas and met many of the Lionni's friends. At one gathering, seated at a long table among many guests in a vineyard, we watched the Perseid meteor shower that lit the sky like the Fourth of July. Frost-dead olive trees were resurrected when they caught the light. Many prosperous Italians Leo knew came from old, respected families. Pietro Stucci's olive oil and restaurants went back generations. His

Roberta Swann

Roman profile could have been etched on old coins. He was intimidating. When I asked a waiter for parmesan to put on his famous pasta, he cut me off, and made me eat more than I wanted in the simple way it was prepared. To break the ice, I told my cinghiali story. He looked at me as if I was crazy. That night, Brian slept with the scorpions.

    A year later, when we were walking along the FDR Drive in Manhattan, watching cormorants, a V of Canada geese flew by. Brian pointed out how the one in front creates an uplift for the ones behind. I pretended not to believe him, though I knew it was true. I said it sounded like another of his cinghiali stories.

House

Then we bought a house. Upstate New York. Delaware County. Autumn Breeze Road. For the first few years we were the only residents, but over the 18 years of ownership each 10-acre lot was sold and built on, one so lavishly it made the cover of *New York Magazine*. For us it was: there goes the neighborhood. We liked it better rough, when we were able to scramble around the empty properties like puppies, running into coyotes, foxes, an albino skunk, even a wolf Brian swears he saw in our back field. We kept a competitive list of animal sightings. He was winning until I ran into a bear shaking blackberries off a bush by the beaver pond I'd taken to visiting each day, hoping to catch another glimpse of their new baby hitching a ride on its mother's tail. My binoculars went black despite my fiddling. When I lowered them, there was the bear standing upright 30 feet away with the posture of a marine. I back-pedalled slowly, as Brian had instructed, and whispered: *Nice bear, handsome boy, enjoy your berries, sorry to disturb you,* retreating gingerly until I hit the red dirt road and ran like hell until I hit our house. "I saw a bear!" I thundered, and pulled out the little red copybook I kept on the kitchen counter and added: *Bear!*

Of course I was afraid, but not as much as I should have been. As our years accumulated in this rural setting, I developed a real feeling for the natural world. Hummingbirds returned each year to our dinky red feeder and deer bedded in the back field. We watched one give birth and saw the baby we called Gemma take her first shaky steps. Turkeys hung out in trees. The grouse I couldn't see exploded noisily under my feet when I got too close. The runaway heifer that jumped over our stone wall and nearly knocked me down belonged to our farm neighbors, the Sanfords, who said: "Oh, that's just Bailey. She follows the deer." Our daily routine included visits to their horses in the field and picking berries, black and blue, off their bushes. They gave us permission to explore their hundreds of beautiful acres. They were a family of original settlers, the Sanfords. I'd often see their names on tombstones in the old cemetery that became a rest stop on my walks. Eva Sanford told us it was her grandfather who named our valley "Vega," after the star in Lyra. A red-tailed hawk grazed my cheek, dive-bombing for a chipmunk who hid in the woodpile, saved but chattering. So many sounds. The lovely thrush versus the thuggish woodpecker who drummed against the metal chimney. Spring peepers and bullfrogs. The red fox who scampered across our deck. The albino skunk who refused to leave our basement. The mink and her babies clicking along the stone wall to get to the goldfish other idiot neighbors stocked their dyed-blue pond with. Who knows why I fell in love with stinkbugs who slow-walked their way across the sun-splashed white oak floor like meditating monks? Or tiny orange efts, defenseless as the newborns they looked like. Luna moths. Field mice. Bats that aren't really as ugly as all that. Well, scary. And maybe a little ugly.

Which reminds me that all was not embraceable. The cluster flies, a million of them, carpeting every surface, had to be swept away every weekend we came up. After the four-hour drive from the city, sweeping flies was not the first thing I wanted to do for the next hour.

In winter, the house took hours to heat. I sat in front of the wood-stove still shivering in my down jacket, waiting to feel warm. When the thermostat kicked in, the house got so hot I ran around in shorts. Brian never felt cold, forever moving in and out, making gardens or putting them to bed, collecting tree-rot or manure by the bucket, really happy in his natural element in any season.

He wanted this country house. I'd been less enthused. But he desired so little, I could hardly protest. Nothing material ever possessed him. When we started our two-year house-hunting, he liked every house we saw. What about that mosquito pond, or the black mold or green and yellow bathroom? I'd ask him. But he was already outside. He loved old barns that took him back to his childhood where he slept in the hayloft above the horses. I vetted the houses, but he saw the land, sensing the past. One house we looked at was so run-down we just walked out back to the barn, still filled with hay. "It smells," I said and Brian smiled. He loved that smell.

We finally compromised on a pretty cottage in the Berkshires that we proceeded to buy and sign paperwork for. In our excitement I never read the fine print and when I did, noticed it was part of a development. All packed and ready to go, we had to unbuy it. We continued our search in the Catskills that very soon after gave us our house and ten acres which my mother, the first time she walked through our fields, called "God's country." We were not well set up to have guests, but had them anyway. I loved the house's emptiness, sleeping on floors, eating on staircases. But surprisingly it was Brian who was eager for a bed. Which led us to Robert's Auction in Fleischmanns.

Robert's was quite an experience. Every Saturday night, the ground floor of his old Catskill hotel filled with 200 people, mostly locals, a few collectors, flinty regulars with reserved seats, and us. Previews were an hour before the seven-o'clock start. Eddie Roberts was a stickler for punctuality and everything else. He was the Don Rickles of auctioneers, quick with insulting comments. When we won the bidding for a small silver hand-warmer, he said to Brian: "You don't look like no hunter to me." Soon after, when we bought a box of farming tools, "nor no farmer, either," he muttered. This was nothing to be proud of in this setting where men stayed rough, and the only grooming they did was reserved for horses. But of course I was fascinated and couldn't get enough, sitting there for six hours until the last lot was sold—everything from broken TVs to a genuine Norman Rockwell scored cooly by the collector from the city who appeared weekly in a white linen suit and a black fedora. We got some great stuff and a basement full of junk. I got hooked on raising my bidding paddle. And on the snack bar that served the worst food that was relished by all. We'd drive back at midnight on pitch-black winding roads to our snug little house, illuminated within like a Halloween pumpkin, buzz the garage door up, then down, and fall into bed. Brian was exhausted. He's not a shopper. I was still excited, anticipating the morning when I'd pore over my bounty. Was I nuts? Why did I buy another nest of baskets? Hankies? Card games? Because they were there.

We never replaced the microwave the nasty seller pulled out of the wall. "I'm not giving this away for nothin'," he told us. So over the hole we hung a temporary linen tea-cloth with yellow chicks breaking out of the shells. For 18 years! Aside from staining the deck, constantly replacing shingles the wind blew off, resurfacing the long steep driveway, fixing an outside staircase, we weren't what you'd call obsessed with improvements. Obsession was reserved for the garden because Brian wouldn't cut down any of his trees. He carved it out of a sunless section and made his own soil. He spent the first two summers collecting manure and tree rot ("duff," he called it) in buckets, making many trips a day, turning over the soil until it was ready for worms. We lived in the area where bluestone comes from and the red hardpan he worked with was full of large flat stones. He used a heavy crowbar to break the soil and lever out slabs he used to build a wall that stretched halfway around the house. Contrary to what Eddie Roberts said, nothing we bought was used for decoration. Especially the scythe Brian used almost daily.

We never developed a passion for bushhogging and kept our acres as they wanted to be. Even our garden had a mind of its own, though Brian did innovate. He hung string from the deck for scarlet runner beans and planted thirty varieties of vegetable seeds. He grew the best Sungold tomatoes anyone's ever tasted. We did have to contend with the tyranny of slugs and deer. The worst, however, was a small red squirrel we christened Big Red, who managed to mangle three state-of-the-art squirrel-proof bird-feeders, and dig up the squash seeds. Even sun-dried laundry was up for grabs. I blamed Big Red for incorporating my panties into his dray. But he lived in a tree-hole. It was the gray squirrel who was guilty. His boldest escapade involved the two dozen bagels I'd brought up from the city that had gone stale. I put them in the compost. We were standing on the deck, watching the sun sink, full of gratitude for Mother Earth, when I spotted three bagels parked up a white pine tree. Brian saw more in the maples. Big Red! This was the stunt that made him a legend.

In retrospect, the house was ethereal. It never sunk in that we owned it. Each time our car turned up the drive, I was surprised it was still there. The broken front door, which we meant to replace, was left unlocked. The deck's screen door was vulnerable. We never put in a security system, and never had a break-in or intruders, like some of our more protected neighbors.

I took long hikes that made everyone nervous. With no tracking skills, I sometimes got lost. "Watch out for the One-

Eyes," an old-timer warned. One-Eyes, he explained, were mountain people who spied from behind trees with one eye. I never saw one. But they couldn't have been more terrifying than the mongrel dogs that once blocked my passage. I took shelter in an abandoned farm-house, praying Brian would sense my danger and come looking for me. He did. There was no cell service in the beautiful Vega Valley. I had to rely on magical thinking.

I didn't take to country life so quickly. There was the comfort factor, for one. It was seriously cold in winter and our wood stove took a while to kick in. And when it did, it was soon too hot. Some summer days were so hot I set up shop in the cooler basement. Then there was the fact that the Transfer Station was some 20 miles away and each week we'd haul all the non-composted rubbish there. After, we'd often stop off at the naturalist John Burrough's house outside Roxbury before returning home. It was preserved as a national landmark and fun to snoop.

There were no decent food shops. Walmart was in Kingston, 90 minutes away. I'd never been to a Walmart, and actually enjoyed the experience of skating down the aisles, filling a huge cart with those packaged goods I'd always avoided, limiting Brian to one industrial-sized bag of purple tortilla chips per trip.

There was no doctor nearby, only a nurse-practitioner who kept banker's hours. The first month we arrived I had a nasty accident. We were in an antique shop when a ten-foot fluorescent fixture fell on my head that was stitched up at the small Margaretville hospital. For some reason, I took this in stride and wore a baseball cap when my mother visited. Six weeks later, when the Indian doctor removed all 45 staples, he asked if I'd like to keep them. "Why would I?" I asked. "Because you paid for them," was his reply.

I did miss city life, my fashion jobs, the Soho weekend routine, running into people and shops. But the house and environs had a strong pull, and by my third summer I could talk local gossip and share animal sightings, dig out of Hurricane Irene, witness spectacular storms, feel more competent and assured in rough circumstances.

One thing that remained unchanged was politics. Even though second-home owners boosted the local economy, there was resentment. Prices for repairs and snow removal doubled for city folk. When we hired someone to re-do our driveway, he gave Brian a $2500 estimate until I interceded and asked: "What can you do for a thousand bucks?" So he did the same job for a thousand, stopping ten feet from our garage door to make his point. Then there was the man who owned the Roxbury hotel, funeral parlor, mini-mart and drugstore who chaired the local council. He was also the man you'd grieve your taxes to if you were silly enough to bother. When we phoned the Town Sheriff to say we had wild dogs on our property he said "Shoot them." We had no gun. But everyone else did. Brian almost got shot by a trespassing hunter who built a blind up an old maple and shrugged off the offense by explaining, "I thought you were a deer." I hated hunting season and was truly unnerved by those gunblasts.

So what did we do with our time? We walked all over following deer tracks, trespassing where we could, picking berries, apples, pears, from old, wild trees, climbing to the weather station, feeding windfall apples to the horses, noticing how each year our small trees grew big enough to block the view of the valley I'd bought the house for.

Our neighbor shot a black bear raiding his bee hives and made the front page of the *Catskill Mountain News*. Along with his wife, Cheryl, he ran Tea Thyme, where they sold their jams and honey. We became friends, and when they came for dinner it turned out bears weren't the only things on Will's hit list: Democrats, deer, beavers, weekenders, gays and anything that kept his wife away from her duties. They'd met in the back pages of a *Survivalist* magazine. She carried a pint-sized revolver in her sports bra whenever she took her dogs on long walks and had used it twice.

*

A film crew was shooting a movie near Margaretville. On the way to Robert's auction we almost ran Christian Slater down. He was walking in the middle of the road in that happy trance I understood. Country walks become refuge. Time collapses. Brian still looked for that wolf he saw our first summer. Some say there are still mountain lions roaming around. The guy who delivered our wood saw one. At the annual Valley Picnic in August, the locals regale each other with such stories while the Wall Street-type newcomers compare construction costs, resale values, ski conditions and whether Kelsey Grammar will stay or sell.

We saw our house re-listed a year after we sold it. Even after it was no longer ours, we referred to it as ours, following its weather conditions on TV. We never met the buyers who said we could leave everything behind, which we did, including a few of Brian's children's books for the owners, which he signed for their children with best wishes, never acknowledged. It's not the house we miss so much as the roots we pulled up. Maybe not completely, though. Brian still gets himself to sleep calling up the crisp cut and motion of the scythe we bought at Eddie's.

We sold the house because Brian was hit by a truck in the city and broke his hip. The long ride up no longer made sense. While he was in the hospital, I phoned an estate agent who got the ball rolling. It took a year to sell. We never met the buyers, a young Indian Wall Street couple with two small children, who annoyed us with petty emails. I wanted the house to go to another couple whose higher bid and passionate connection to the place made me feel I was passing it over to people who could continue our journey. But legalities prevailed. The first couple got the house at a lower price and put it up for sale a year later.

A Seat on the Bus

That's how it started. A young woman catches my eye, offers her seat. I feign a smile and shake my head. I *am* tired, but screw her. Do I look as if I'm ready to keel over? My reflection in the dirty window looks like it always looks. Like me. I'm dressed to impress. Maybe not to the uneducated. But the fashion crew I work with admire my uncommon taste, know my oversize coat is Isabel Marant and the rough edges purposeful. I'm only on for two stops anyway so continue to stand in a soldiery way.

"What would you do if someone offered you a seat?" I ask Sylvia, my dentist, friend and contemporary. "I'd take it," she says and continues sandblasting my teeth. Her answer, like a trip up the mountain. Why didn't I react like that? I'm not silly or vain, not a woman who needs a lot of pampering, don't dress to attract notice, and wear clever clothes mostly for fun. Beauty is exuberance. Blake said that. Maybe that moment on the bus meant the gig was up. I can no longer pull off 40 for 50 or 50 for 60. Pretension to youthfulness is absurd anyway. So maybe that seat offer finally caught up with me. *Hey, what took you so long?*

When I get home and tell Brian, he slings his arm around me. We sit down for a talk. I put on my listening face. He boils the perils of aging down to invisibility and loss of power. I disagree. I just returned a very expensive gift to Barney's without a receipt. I challenge anyone, radiant with youth, to do that.

A lot has been confirmed about aging. Said neatly, we are

programmed to decline. Worse is what some women do to counter that. Like the Ms. Senior America Pageant, billed as a place where beauty and age converge, held in Atlantic City and Las Vegas. Where else? Contestants spend $2000 to enter, not counting the cost of beaded gowns and sparkling tiaras. Sharon from Wyoming wants you to know she's 73 and still a sexy blonde. Ethel tap-dances, but Mandy has her beat with a go-go routine. All summarize their philosophy of life in 35 seconds. There is no swimsuit competition. But the *Barbra Streisand Songbook* gets a workout. The women on stage sway to a song written especially for them: "The Little Girl Inside." Tears and cheers abound. This is not a tough audience.

Am I alone to despise this? It makes me feel the crazy I felt after the election. The more I listen to Trump, the less terrible death begins to seem. Old age is not a safe place. It's easy to appear foolish. Blythe Danner should not shill laxatives. Tony Bennett might pull back a bit. The 98 year-old yoga teacher—give it a rest. When yoga felt like another errand, I quit.

My dance with age continues. Before I leave the house I ask my husband: Hat or no hat? He pulls a beanie down on my head with a mother's touch. I've made concessions. Don't run around the city anymore looking like Robin Hood wearing racy Lululemon outfits. I neither want to age gracefully nor disgracefully. Feel more natural with makeup than without. And agree with Oscar Wilde who said looking natural is an irritating pose. Maybe getting old is the surprise it shouldn't be, because of all those small magpie thefts along the way. Still, the puzzle of why, when a seat is offered, I refuse to take it, remains unresolved, I think.

MISS BROOKLYN

A news photo of the Flatbush Loew's Theater being refurbished and landmarked brought me back to my sixteen year-old self. My best friend Zelda and I were contestants in the Miss Brooklyn Beauty Contest. Zelda was slim and sexy, from Poland. I was just cute. We were inseparable. When I'd walk her home she'd walk me back. We'd stroll the streets collecting wolf-whistles. But as close as we were, I still loaded her after-school baloney sandwiches with mayonnaise and too much meat, hoping she'd get fat. We'd met in seventh grade. I was in Honor English. She spoke with an accent. We were both outsiders in our own ways. She, an immigrant, slow to learn. I, without a father, a father I reincarnated at times, pretending at summer camp he was fighting in Cuba. *Cuba?* To Zelda I told the truth. Her family became mine— Zelig and Anna Kartowski, her father and mother; Pinkus, aka Pinky, and Robert, her very bad little brothers. Their kitchen was always filled with bakery boxes. Zelig was always trying to kiss me. Anna ran after the boys with a strap. But when caught she'd cover them with kisses. I helped everyone with homework and wrote letters to relatives in Poland. They treated me like a little star. The boiling pans and boisterous pranks were welcome relief from the solemn atmosphere at home. My mother was a widow who suffered enough, so I kept a low profile. With the Kartowskis I drank vodka, wore miniskirts and tube tops, ate *chaserei* and felt giddy.

    Zelda won Miss Brooklyn. She was really beautiful. I was jealous. All that mayonnaise only made her olive skin glow more. She shared her prize money and we bought ten outfits for a hundred bucks at May's department store. The category BFF was not yet born, but we never thought we wouldn't be friends forever.

SHE HAS SOME NERVE

She stopped into Williams Sonoma to buy his favorite Medicis White Almonds. As she exited, a salesman plugging the new Nespresso machine buttonholed her, wondering if she'd like a cup. *If she didn't have to wait. Could he make it a cappuccino?* He foams the milk. Good, but not sweet enough. *Some sugar?* He offers a packet. She leaves, sipping, skipping the sales pitch. Still a bit bitter. She dips into Starbucks and helps herself to a Splenda. Perfect. The jolt is exactly what she needed. Her pace quickens. She feels full of herself. She has some nerve. She can't wait to tell him.

There's Always Free Cheese in a Mousetrap

Twice, 8H stole 8G's packages. Once, it was a Fresh Express delivery, and 8G went without their vegetarian dinner. When confronted, 8H denied the theft and later slipped a newsclip under 8G's door that confirmed crime was up in the 13th Precinct. This was from an older woman who'd just had her husband arrested for sexual assault, who, while he was in jail, belted out arias and looked happier than I'd ever seen her.

I met her on the elevator. She was biting into an apple. "I just wanted to tell you," she said, "I share my fruit and wine." I was a little charmed. Maybe the mezuzah on her door meant something. Maybe she was just an eccentric. When her husband, who resembled Ichabod Crane, returned, he looked less skeletal. The young couple in 8G were convinced she starved him.

Later that week, I found a bag hanging on my doorknob. Inside was a chef's salad locked in a plastic clamshell I cut my finger opening. As I tossed the wilted lot, a label fell to my feet. 8H, it said. That took care of the "eccentric" thing.

Red and Blue

I missed the red thong I lost in the wash. But how? It's only he and I, alone, in our home away from home. Then, a season later, cleaning up the garden, a flash of red led me to the squirrel's fallen nest where, woven into the weave, was my weathered underwear. Like the blue beach-pail I lost in the sand then found in the snow, which confirmed there are places for everything.

Birthday

for Brian on his 60-something

"I like to know what everybody's up to,"
he says, shaking a trowel, taking
another turn around the tomatoes, looking
a little like Brando at the end
of the movie that never ended.

In favorite pjs, worn for weeks,
dug out again from laundry
I haven't washed, he's happy.
Why not? He made soil from scratch.
His worms are fat and there's a lot
of them.

He loves his garden–
a division of labor.
He plants, waters, weeds, and waits
on me. And I allow him.
Except tonight. I'm taking him out.

But the restaurant has moved
since last year. I should have phoned.
We make the long ride home.
Even the radio has nothing to say.
Then, turning up our drive,
we startle a treeful of—
"Oh, look!" I say. "Roasting turkeys!"
They flutter, fly, run, scatter, squawk

Roberta Swann

and sound so much like *Surprise!*
But it's a flock of crows
pecking at his heirlooms again
that make him jump out of the car
shouting and waving. And from where
I sit, peering into the side mirror
where things appear more *festive*
than they really are,
it looks like a party to me.

Thrushes

How on earth, he asks, did ants
get inside the hummingbird feeder
hanging from a wire in thin air?
They're ants, I say. That's what they do.
Sniff out sweets, even the stash
under my underwear. He's having none
of it, still bugged by the varmint
who dug up his garden again.
He tells crows to shut it.
I like crows. They are what they are.
Unlike the chipmunk, pretending
she just *found* those squash seeds.

Prints in the soil. He says bear.
I say skunk, like the one we spotted
shuffling between collards and kale,
picking up bits of this and that.
We hush when turkeys explode
in the woods. I grab his hand.
Maybe bear. He squeezes. *Could
have been skunk.* In the dusk,
hermit thrushes have the last word,
calling to each other.

Roberta Swann

Happy Days

The bagel you're eating.
Put it down. Those pants look
like you were raised in an ashram.
Ashcan? I'll only eat two halves.
You want your Kate and Edith
too. I'm in the mood for something.
Is it almost time to dine?
Die? There's Hamlet in all of us.
You sound like you're onto something,
sir. I always wanted to call him
Sir. Mr. Chips? Chips, chips,
dati, dati, boom, chaboom, chaboom.
It's wonnerful, it's wonnerful.
Good luck, my baby! It's good
to get out of your mind. Those
squash leaves are grand and wave
just like the Queen. That rain
made a big splash until the sun
got into the game. Better than
Brooklyn summers with hydrants
blowing. And that gym teacher
out on parole. Do you like
those blonde sparks in my hair?
Good clothes compose me.
Your pants are entirely wrong.
Did you take your pills?
I treasure our talks.
I can't get a word in

edgewise. If you understand
it's fair game you're wrong.
Wouldn't you say?
Come back soon.

Roberta Swann

Pooh

Shingles are loose.
Water leaks through the roof.
My husband calls Lenny the carpenter,
who, when last he worked for us,
spent more time talking wildlife
and the art of wood
than just getting down to it.
My husband likes Lenny.
They exchange hawk tales
and local dust-ups.
I like less mouth, more hammer,
figured Lenny right away
too dashing for the job.

He arrives inconveniently early.
Doesn't bring his big ladder.
And can't do this on his own.
Or in the next few weeks.
But, he says, no worries.
A tarp will catch the coming rain,
and did I tell you about the bear
I saw in my backwoods, really *saw*?
Not every day you see a bear
that deep up close.

I watch Lenny growl and make faces,
playing both parts. "You got nothin',"
says the bear, advancing

to retreat and, bingo, slides
to sit against a tree
like Winnie the Pooh.

I don't say a word.
Later fetch a bucket,
opting to keep my marriage together,
unlike the roof.

Roberta Swann

Owl

Not mad for birthdays, I cash in
on the storm and stay inside, watching
branches jump up and down.

Even at five, blowing out fires
wasn't my thing. I'd rather play
Dead Indian, popping up for another go.

Just when rain seems it will never end,
it does. Hummingbirds bomb feeders
chasing sugar-highs and I think about

baking a cake, but who am I kidding?
I sit under a tree instead, and oh, you
hermit thrush, I see you singing your

good time. Shouldn't I be pushing
down sorrow? How happy can
another birthday be? When the owl

enters the picture, I have my answer.

An American Classic

It's the Tenth Annual Vega Valley Picnic.
A red white and blue sheet cake says so.
Neighbors bring covered dishes and kiss
like they see each other more than once a year.
For once in my life I have someone to lean on....
Can't get that song out of my head until I unplug
and my husband steers me to the stories
lobbing back and forth like tennis balls.
I still get mileage from the bear I saw up close,
summers ago. Mostly, I sit like an owl,
a mesmerized listener, catching the jam and mustard man
saying business got so bad he thought dammit
was God's last name. But do you really want to hear that?
Stay with me. Because I'm noticing how some age
and some don't, like there's two price-lists
for getting old. And how one Mary doubled her size
and the other halved hers. Take my word.
I've always been a fat-check girl.
It's four p.m. now. Equal parts day and night.
I'm sitting at a table where a local lady
slides slices of cake to everyone but me
so I get up to see what remains
of the food and find a gummy orange casserole
I'm glad isn't mine that only the old gray dog
has eyes for. *Silence of the yams,* I dub
to myself and Stevie Wonder-ful singing duets.
Rain starts. Sounds jazzy. Fills from a guitar
I like. People shift, except for a kid

Roberta Swann

with crazy yellow hair who keeps tumbling
on the grass and tells me it's her birthday,
and I tell my husband in the car I think
I forgot something. "To eat," he says.
"Would it kill you once in your life to eat?"
He doesn't sound sore or sing out of tune.
Someone, someone, someone who needs me.

Trash Talk

Kanye says:
To not show Kim naked
would be like birds not singing.
So it's a quiet night in the news cycle
and she's wearing a crazy cat's-cradle
of a dress, oiled and ready for the spit.

She's no little-ass girl.
She loves herself. Girls,
greedy for glamour.
Can't get enough of her—
a giant lollipop you can't finish.
Fake fruit by the foot.

She's a big girl by any standard;
Generates interest by doing nothing.
How big is her closet?
Which house?

Roberta Swann

STAYING ALIVE

My father, who died at 38, when I was 12, always called me "the Kid." "How was the Kid today?" he'd ask my mother when he came home from work. My mother had scolded me many times for bad behavior, warning: Just wait till your father gets home. But now she just said *fine* when I was only OK.

    I keep his dog tags, service medals and army patches in a box on my desk and still pore over them. He keeps me company every day: The lucky pennies he taught me to covet I still pick up. My bad dreams were stopped by his Bible with US Army insignia under my pillow. My early cancer was caught because he left a letter to every member of his family to get a yearly check-up.

    He still has plans for me: My good luck from the other side. Even now, when losses and failures accumulate, I keep luck small. I lose my keys. And find them again.

Windfall

We stuff pockets with plastic bags
for windfall apples gathered
beyond our back field.

Some days are as simple as apples,
filling a few bags, leaving some for the deer
who might have left them for us.

About the Author

ROBERTA SWANN's poetry and fiction have appeared in many journals, including *Kenyon Review, North American Review, Ploughshares, College English, Indiana Review, The Village Voice, The American Voice, Alaska Review, The New York Times,* and so on. Of her most recent book, *Everything Happens Suddenly,* Mary Oliver wrote that the poems "are deft and full of charm and humor, a mixture of dark and light—the embrace of all of it. That is her special gift."

She has taught at The Cooper Union, The Bennington Writing Workshops, Indiana University, The New School, Baruch College, Cape Cod Writers' Conference, and Poets and Writers. She has been in residence at the McDowell Colony and the Dorland Mountain Colony. She appears in *Who's Who in American Women, The New Grove Dictionary of Jazz,* and elsewhere. For fifteen years she was Director of Public Programs at Cooper Union's Great Hall, where she co-founded The American Jazz Orchestra.

www.ingramcontent.com/pod-product-compliance
Lightning Source LLC
Chambersburg PA
CBHW020332170426
43200CB00006B/361